PRIMUM NON NOCERE

Copyright © 2017, David C. Stone

All rights reserved. This book or any portion thereof
may not be reproduced or used in any manner whatsoever
without the express written permission of the publisher.

Second Printing, 2017

ISBN-13: 978-1500778750
ISBN-10: 1500778753

PREFACE

The stories presented throughout this book outline a ten year period of my journey in emergency medical services from volunteering to working as a paramedic. The events are real, although some details have been changed to protect the identity of those involved.

The purpose of this book is not to glorify myself through high-intensity, adrenalin packed war stories. It is to expose the reader to the harsh reality of managing a dynamic, fast-paced emergency scene and how these encounters have a lasting impact on the responder.

The stories I chose to present had the largest emotional impact in my life. They changed me from the person I used to be and shaped me into who I am today. These are the experiences that will stay with me forever.

There is no intention to discredit the emergency services field. A book detailing the thousands of patients I attended where everything went right would not be a compelling read. The experiences in this book provided the framework that made me a good medic.

DAVID C. STONE
AUTHOR

I am husband and father of four young children. I had been involved in emergency services since I was eighteen. I ended my service as a Paramedic to spend more time with my family and live a more meaningful life. I am not an author. I initially wrote about my calls as a coping mechanism to deal with the stress I was facing. Although I did not like the path emergency services had taken my life, what I learned throughout my career ultimately changed me into who I am today. I wrote this book to share my experience in hopes it could help others in ways I may not yet understand.

STORIES

VOLUNTEER 1

    A Perspective on Life 3

    The White Paper 5

    Peaceful Death 8

    Standing in the Corner 14

    Officer Down 17

    Change of Heart 22

EMERGENCY MEDICAL TECHNICIAN 27

    What's The Worst Thing You've Ever Seen 29

    Don't Say Needles 32

    Little Shits 36

    Right of Way 43

    Falling Off a Cliff 47

    Your Call, Buddy 52

    Reassurance 56

PARAMEDIC SCHOOL 59

    No Crying on the Ambulance 61

    Invisible Boy 71

    Day of The Falls 76

    An Angel's Halo 82

    The Most Stable Rhythm 86

    Training Day 92

PARAMEDIC ... 97

Campfire Ghost Stories ... 99

Almost a Bad Day ... 102

You'll Never Be the Last One ... 107

If She Dies, She Dies ... 116

Four Loco ... 120

When You Start Thinking About Your Kids ... 125

The Golden Hour ... 129

Monday Morning Quarterback ... 133

Nightmares ... 138

The Real World ... 142

Sixth Sense ... 148

Tough Guys ... 153

That's Already Been Done ... 158

Careful What You Wish For ... 161

One Day Later ... 164

Possessed ... 172

Primum Non Nocere ... 179

The Closest Unit ... 184

Ambulance Drivers ... 189

Hands of an Angel ... 194

What's The Best Call You've Ever Had? ... 197

Today Was a Good Day ... 199

VOLUNTEER

A Perspective on Life

The smell of airbag deployment that fills the passenger compartment from a head on collision down a quiet country road. The gurgle of vomiting when performing CPR on a dead stranger. The screams from a young child who just saw the dead body of her mother. All of these describe ugliness to me. These have been my experiences since I decided to become an EMT.

When I was seventeen, I might have had a different definition of ugliness. But now, I have a new perspective. I would define ugliness as the utmost state of pain and misery people experience.

I have seen the lifeless body of a woman whose vehicle got split in half on the interstate. I have seen the outline in grass which was preserved from burning by its homeowner. I have seen a helicopter fly away with a little girl who likely won't survive her crushing dirt bike accident. I have seen the result of drunk driving. I have heard a man scream to God for forgiveness while he was pinned underneath his rolled over vehicle. I have seen the heartbreak of those who lost a friend to a drug deal gone wrong. I have seen the anger in family members when we were unable to resuscitate their loved ones.

But, I have not seen it all.

I had no idea that much ugliness actually existed. It is real, and it is my definition of ugly because I have witnessed it repeatedly. Anyone who joins the field of emergency medicine for the excitement and adrenalin rush is in for a rude awakening.

Life is ugly.

THE WHITE PAPER

I used to care what other people thought. I was once self-conscious and nervous about the attention brought upon me. That really only made me appear more awkward, attempting to hide in plain sight surrounded by others. I hated being the center of attention. I talked less, mainly because the less I spoke the less I was noticed. At least I thought. I was nervous at the thought of having to speak in front of others. During high school, I remained inside a shell counting down the days until graduation. That would be my day of freedom. Free from judgment and free from ridicule.

I held all my thoughts within. On the outside I looked hopeless and destine to live a life playing video games alone in my parent's basement. On the inside, I had a vision and a plan for something different. I wanted my life to be better than it was. After the terrorist attacks on US soil, I finally understood where I wanted to take my life.

On September 11, 2001, I sat in a classroom with twenty-some other students, all with our eyes glued to the television set. We were trying to comprehend what had just happened. We were wondering if the world we were used to was going to change forever. I watched as the men and women of FDNY raced towards the burning towers in a courageous attempt to save countless victims. I was infatuated with the heroism demonstrated when suddenly my teacher turned off the TV.

"That's enough of that. We still have to have school today," she told the class.

I didn't learn a thing that day from my educators. I was pissed at them for shutting off what was surely history in the making. A desire to help began fueling me. I finally knew what I wanted to do with my life.

My father was a Lieutenant with the fire department in our rural town. For years, he had been trying to convince my brother and me to volunteer, but so far had been unsuccessful. The year after the attacks, I enrolled in a cadet program offered through my high school for fire suppression and emergency medical aid. My brother, who must have felt the same desire I had, joined the department that year.

As soon as I was eligible, I began volunteering for the same department my dad and brother were involved with. After passing the regional training academy, I was placed on their shift.

The events written within *'A Perspective on Life'* encompassed my first two years in emergency services. As part of a college writing course, I was assigned to discuss the topic of *ugliness*. With my recent exposure to this side of life, I found the subject quite fitting.

I have no recollection of my first response. I can only recall the excitement that circulated my body as the alarms in our station rang. Someone needed me and I was equipped to handle their emergency.

I prepared mentally and physically for the title and knew I would not let stress get in the way of my passion. I was not going to end up a statistic of those who could not handle the pressure of an emergency.

I looked up to my station Captain who could scrape body parts off the highway and return to the station to eat lunch like it was nothing.

In reality, nothing had prepared me for the horrific scenes I was destined to face. The thrill overpowered the emotion of the events and in an eerie way I desired more. I became obsessed. It was a high I continued to chase, but would never get back. Once the thrill was gone, all that was left was the emotion. I held it deep inside.

I used to be easy-going. I used to not get frustrated or angry. I used to maintain a level head and think my way through problems. I used to not have anxiety over small situations. I used to be able to cope with life. I used to have compassion and concern for others. I used to be a good person. That all changed once I became a paramedic.

PEACEFUL DEATH

"I HAVE SEEN THE LIFELESS BODY OF A WOMAN WHOSE VEHICLE GOT SPLIT IN HALF ON THE INTERSTATE..."

I took pride in the work I did as a volunteer and held it to a higher regard than my actual job. Although, a minimum wage position was all that would hire me at the time, I believed I was better than it. I made my employer work their schedule around my fire rotations. I had no concern over showing up to work late and unannounced, only to have the excuse that I was mitigating some local disaster.

Luckily, I had the support of management who understood that the position I held was only a stepping stone. Working in retail was where I earned my money but not where my heart was. They appreciated my excitement for volunteering and were happy I was out there helping others in need.

I was dressing up in khakis and polo for work when the pager went off. I was really not looking forward to another day of cashiering, so the tones came as a relief. Our department was severely understaffed and became desperate for help when a major incident occurred. Although our Chief Officers stressed that our priorities should be family first, then our job, and then the department, I was ready to push my job last if the call was right.

"ALS motor vehicle accident, southbound I-5, semi truck versus vehicle," dispatch reported.

My job could wait. I needed to be on this call.

My dad was already heading out to his truck to assist the response. I ran out in the driveway, grabbed bunker gear from the trunk of my car, and rushed toward him.

"Don't you have to go to work?" he questioned me.

"I'll just tell them I was stuck on a call. They won't care."

He didn't seem too concerned. I had already made up my mind and he knew I would have to deal with any consequences. There was a major incident occurring and no time for discussion. We drove down the street to an unmanned station which housed a fire engine. After donning our gear, we hopped in the engine and took off toward the scene.

Dispatch updated us, "Multiple vehicles involved, possible entrapment, one patient is unconscious." The update had me excited. I was eager to see the carnage on scene and be able to help the victims. In my head, there was only a happy ending. We would rush in, utilize our skills, and save a life. I was new in the department and had not seen any real action since I had joined. The thrill was overpowering.

We arrived soon after the first incoming unit. The Captain who assumed Command had his firefighters sorting out the scene and identifying the most critical victims. Besides the semi, there looked to be three other vehicles involved with pretty heavy damage. I grabbed trauma equipment as I stepped off the engine and followed my dad into the scene. He met up with Command to get an update and orders.

"We have one dead in that vehicle," Command briefs my dad, pointing to one of the heavily damaged cars blocking the middle lanes of the interstate. He skips over the second heavily damaged vehicle and focuses on the semi. "She went across the median and was struck by the semi. The guy in the semi is okay. There's a van over there with damage. There are four occupants inside that haven't been looked at yet. So, I am going to send you guys over there to check them out for now."

I felt the need to say something about the second vehicle with heavy damage but figured he had the situation handled. I was only a probie. I was expected to follow orders with my mouth shut and ears open. Quietly, I hauled our equipment over to the van. I couldn't help but stare inside at the four elderly women who were obviously shaken up from the collision. My dad walked around the van inspecting for damage as he glanced at the patients within.

"David, open the door and talk to them. Find out what their injuries are," he tells me.

I open the big sliding door on the passenger side and ask each occupant if they are alright. I didn't even notice my dad had left to report back to Command.

"How are you guys doing?" I ask the group. They looked at me as if my casual question made me the most insensitive prick in the world. I didn't know what else to say. I was only concerned about their condition and needed a way to get information from the four of them quickly. Their vehicle had been traveling down the freeway when the car from the opposite side crossed and struck the semi. Their van was a secondary collision with that of the dead woman's vehicle. Even though they didn't take the direct impact, they still had pretty extensive damage to the side door. The passenger sitting closest to the impact appeared to be in more pain than everyone else.

The Captain in command and my dad both approach me as I was attempting to assess multiple victims. I was used to dealing with one simulated patient in EMT class. The rest of the scene fought for my attention causing me to have difficulty focusing on my assessment skills.

"Are they injured?" Command asks me. "Do they need to be backboarded?"

I felt doubtful in my overall assessment, but the answer still seemed to come clear. It didn't take months of schooling or experience to tell who was the most critical. In my heart, I knew who needed to go first. With a look of confidence, I tell him, "The one in the rear passenger seat needs to come out first. She's the worst."

"Are the rest going to need to be transported?" he asks me.

"I'm not sure, yet. They seem shaken up but I don't know if they have injuries yet."

The Captain looks at me for a second, notes the confidence in my decision and says, "Alright, you got a backboard?"

I work on placing the patient in immobilization equipment with a few other firefighters. I felt nervous being put on the spot but was relieved that this instance worked out for me. I knew I needed moments like this to prove my skill and abilities to the senior members of the department. Even though I felt unsure of myself, I believed I portrayed confidence to those in charge of me. I had such a desire to succeed that I developed an ability to fake it until I made it. I used to be so nervous that I could barely talk or function when I was put on the spot. Something was different here. I felt like a new person. I felt the power than came with the position and it gave me the boost I needed to perform. One call at a time, I was furthering my experience and would only get better.

"Jake," my dad addresses Command by his first name. "What else can we do for you?"

"Everyone's been transported that needs to go. That car is DOA, the semi driver has been cleared no aid needed..."

I couldn't help but notice that the commanding officer in charge of the scene has failed to mention anything about the second vehicle with heavy damage for the second time now. I couldn't take it any longer. I had to interrupt.

"Has anyone checked that car over there?"

"Where?" Command questions me.

I point to the mangled piece of metal sitting thirty yards further down the freeway from the vehicle containing the body. "That hatchback over there, further past the fatality."

"That thing?" he says, confused by my questioning at first. "That's the other half of the fatality's car."

"What?" I respond in shock. I take a few steps closer in an attempt to get a better look. The cars are so mangled it is difficult to tell what end is which.

"That used to be a station wagon," Command continues explaining. "It got hit so hard it split in half from the impact. There's no one else in it. We already checked."

I sat stunned. *Holy shit! That used to be one car?*

Personnel from the fire department continued cleaning up equipment. I assisted them while soaking in the entire picture of the scene. While packing up, I ran the scenario through my head. The woman drove down the same stretch of freeway I had traveled many times before, only to cross somehow and have her life ended in a split second.

As the scene wrapped up, my dad approached me and asked, "Did you get a chance to see the station wagon up close yet?"

"No," I tell him.

"Have you seen a dead person before?" he asks.

"No. Not yet," I say apprehensively. It was only a matter of time before this moment would become reality, but my mind could still not comprehend what was about to happen. Horrific images raced through my imagination in fear of what I was going to be exposed to.

Together, father and son, we walk to the car. He partially removes the tarp covering the body of the driver. Inside is a woman who looks to be in her thirties. She appears unusually peaceful. Her eyes stare to the right and up towards the sky. There are no obvious wounds visible. There is no blood. It really wasn't as bad as I expected. The ghostly white shade of her skin and lack of muscle tone made it clear she was deceased. Her body remained in position only from her skeletal frame and seatbelt. I stood there staring as the tarp gets placed back over her.

STANDING IN THE CORNER

"THE SCREAMS FROM AN ELEMENTARY-AGED GIRL WHO JUST SAW THE DEAD BODY OF HER MOTHER..."

I learned early in my career that life can be fragile. My world was so easy in comparison to those I kept responding to. I was raised sheltered and protected. I only knew my own life. I had no recollection of death in the family, because my grandparents passed when I was very young. Any troubles that happened within the family were kept from me. I was the youngest and protected from experiencing any pain or discomfort.

I could not imagine living the life of those who experienced misery at such a young age. It showed me that this dream I had been living could be shattered at any moment.

We got a call for a possible unconscious woman found in bed. It was past noon and unusual for her to be sleeping. Her daughter called 911 after being unable to wake her. I rode on the engine with our volunteer Chaplin, who was also a trained firefighter and EMT. With medical bags in hand, we were met at the door by a ten year old girl.

I didn't know what to think, so I followed the lead of my Chaplin. Being naive, I rushed in with the little girl closely behind. My focus was solely on the patient and not on controlling the scene. We headed down a long hallway to a back bedroom. I was confused to find a woman lying peacefully in her bed.

A sense of relief set over me. I placed my medical kit on the ground thinking she was only sleeping. I was hoping to get to use some of my skills, but I was also relieved that this little girl was not going to find her mom dead. The Chaplin approached the side of the bed. The woman was lying on her stomach with her head facing away from us. I pictured us waking her up from a deep sleep and her daughter breathing a sigh of relief. The Chaplin knew better.

"Ma'am! Ma'am! Are you awake?" he shouts as he jolts her body. No response.

"Help me roll her!" he shouts.

My heart sank. I didn't know what I was going to do. Without thinking any further I jumped into action, following the orders given to me. I grasp the lady and helped roll her onto her back. Her rigid body held the same position she fell asleep in. Rigor mortis caused her stiff arms to suspend above her body. As we expose this horrific sight, I hear a scream from the corner of the room. I quickly look back to see the little girl in the doorway with her hands covering her mouth. Her eyes were wide open, fixated on the cold, stiff body of her mother. She turned around and ran back into the living room.

The Chaplin paused, set down his equipment, and followed the daughter of the deceased. I put a sheet over the woman's body but sat there for a bit to avoid the scene in the next room. It was a strange feeling hanging out with the dead to avoid the living. I didn't know how to respond to the situation. I didn't know what to say. I I felt like there was nothing I could do to console her. Deep inside, I wanted intense calls to respond to, but I never thought of how it would impact their loved ones.

Officer Down

"I HAVE SEEN THE RESULT OF DRUNK DRIVING..."

Pushing down any emotional involvement, I still found it exhilarating running calls. Not every response was dramatic, but the dull moments only had me craving for more excitement. I was quickly being immersed in the crazy world of emergency services and loved it. The fun part was sharing war stories with friends. It was safe and exciting re-living the thrill of the call after the conclusion had already been determined. During the actual call, it really was not fun. It was scary and nerve racking. There were too many variables that hadn't unfolded yet. The future was unknown and there was no telling what would happen.

I never anticipated being in danger while responding on calls. Scene safety was a major emphasis in our training, but the understanding was that police would secure the scene before we entered. The problem was that the scene could change at any moment. The textbook alone could not prepare us for real life. Experience taught me that I had to be on my toes on every incident. I entered the field thinking it was fun and games, but that thought was quick given a reality check.

I've always been a deep sleeper. I constantly worried that I would miss the tones in the middle of the night while I was on shift. I didn't want to miss out on the action. I also didn't want our station Captain being disappointed in me for failing to perform.

I woke up. The lights in the dorm were on and a voice was talking through the speaker on the ceiling. My mind was cloudy and my body was begging me to go back to sleep. It took a while to comprehend what was happening. I sat up in bed and finally my brain kicked in enough to realize we had a call.

I ran out to the apparatus bay where the guys from my shift were already putting on their bunker gear. I followed, stepped into the back of the engine, and put my headset on.

"What are we going on?" I ask the crew.

Everyone was still waking up, just as I was, although they seemed more attentive. "It's a motor vehicle accident. One car rollover. Unknown injuries."

We roll toward the scene until we find an abandoned vehicle on its top in the ditch. Our red and white emergency lights gave sporadic visibility of the crash scene as we slowly rolled by. There was no patient within. Reports came in that our patient was walking down the road further past our location.

Riding backward in the engine gave me a limited view ahead of us. The engineer and Lieutenant up front were handling the logistics of the call, but I badly wanted to be involved. I stretched my head around to gain a better view. We began creeping up on a man staggering down the shoulder of the quiet country road. This was our patient.

The engine came to a stop and we all stepped out. My dad and brother approach the man first. I began gathering equipment, but could hear profanities being yelled at them. I knew we needed to be cautions as the man was obviously agitated. I glanced over to make sure everyone was still safe. An occasional flash of light revealed blood coming from the patient's face while our guys kept a safe distance.

I met up with the rest of our crew who was slowly following the patient as he continued walking down the road.

"Just be careful. He doesn't want anyone near him and he's pretty aggressive," my dad warns us. "We're going to keep an eye on him and wait for the sheriff's department to assist us in taking him down if we need to."

We followed the patient along the roadway for another few minutes. Between spurts of shouting, he finally stopped in a clearing, turned around and began urinating in the bushes. He was obviously disoriented. The problem was, there was no telling if he was altered from intoxication or head injury. It could be both. There was no doubt he would need to go to the hospital, especially after what he had done to his vehicle.

After what seemed like a long wait, one sheriff vehicles finally arrives. The deputy puts on his black gloves and advances toward the patient in a convincing manner.

"You, stop!" the deputy commands. With a lit cigarette in his mouth and an angry glare the patient stops walking and turns towards the voice. The deputy marches in, but stops a few feet away after closing distance.

"Take the cigarette out of your mouth!" the Sheriff demands.

"Fuck you," is the reply.

This isn't going to go well, I think, watching the scene unfold from behind the cover of law enforcement.

The deputy takes a step in and grabs the patient. The patient fights back and suddenly the deputy is forced to the ground on his back with the patient on top. Without a second thought, I drop my trauma bag and began sprinting toward the chaos. The rest of our company had already swarmed in with the same thought running through their heads: protect the deputy.

Within seconds, the four of us rush the intoxicated man forcing him off the deputy. He ends up face down in the dirt with his arms clenched underneath his chest. I put weight on the guy's back to force him on the ground. Along with me, my brother and one of our firefighters who was an Army veteran hold the guy down until more deputies arrive.

Taking a look back to check on the deputy, I notice he has a deformed ankle. As his adrenalin wears off, he begins shouting in pain.

My dad, the Lieutenant on the engine, gets on the radio and announces, "We have an officer down. Send more law enforcement and one additional aid unit. Have the aid unit standby on arrival."

We had the patient controlled, which was a relief because responses to our rural location could be extensive. Luckily, time seemed to fly by as a flood of blue lights filled the once quiet section of country road.

Black uniforms and badges quickly crowded the scene. "Make room!" a deputy shouts as he approaches. I scoot over and with a swift motion the weight of a burly deputy who came to do business came crushing down on the patient. The sheriff grabbed at the man's arm but he was still able to resist. With all of his might, the deputy could not get the arm to budge. Years of Tae Kwon Do and Muay Thai throughout my childhood was finally going to pay off. I slid my hand under the patient's torso and found his hand buried underneath his body. I reach in and grabbed at the thumb and palm. I started twisting the wrist as hard as I could until it released. I was going to break it if I had to. This man had done enough damage and needed to be subdued. Through my efforts, the arm came right out and the deputy quickly secured it behind his back.

"Nice job," the Sheriff tells me quietly.

I nod silently in response. Inside I was cheering. On the outside, I kept composure as if it were nothing.

Two other deputies force the man's other arm behind his back and finally have him secured with handcuffs. The fight and threat are over.

Months later, the injured deputy stopped by the station while our crew was on duty. We reminisced about the call that brought us together. We got to the point where the deputy was brought down by the patient.

The deputy laughed a bit. "Man, that was a big guy," he began. "I knew he was going to be an asshole, but you know I'm not a small guy myself. I thought I could handle him. I didn't think he would take me down like that."

"The four of us. I know, we weren't expecting that either," Cory, the Army vet says. "We were just staring at you guys like, well shit, he just took out the officer on scene, so we all just jumped on him."

"I was down to my last option," the Sheriff said. "I had my gun out. I don't know if you guys saw, but at that point if he continued attacking me I was going to have to shoot him."

Suddenly the realization of how close our patient was to being killed right in front of us was evident. I also worried about how the call could have gone different. What if the deputy didn't see us rush in and we were caught in the crossfire? What if the patient had a weapon in hand and we rushed in blindly only to get injured or killed ourselves? It angered me that we were placed in that situation. I didn't give a fuck about the patient. My priorities were me, my crew, and the deputy. I was just thankful that this time it all worked out.

The deputy continued, "I'm glad you guys were there and didn't hesitate to take him down. That could have been a really bad situation."

Change of Heart

"I have heard a man scream to God for forgiveness while he was pinned underneath his rolled over vehicle..."

I learned many hard lessons about drinking and driving during my initial years volunteering due to the high volume of alcohol-related incidents we responded to. "Don't drink and drive," was a phrase you heard redundantly until the point almost lost its meaning. Seeing the result first hand was more than enough to convince anyone to stay away from the mixture. Ironically though, the scenes experienced in this field only brought you closer to the substance.

   I arrived to my shift earlier than any other member. Our department was primarily volunteer with one career staff member assigned daily. We frequently were left with gaps in coverage between temporary employees leaving shift and volunteers arriving when they could. The system wasn't perfect, but we made it work the best we could. As I was preparing my bunker gear in the apparatus bay, the tones went off for a rollover motor vehicle accident deep on one of our back roads. Reports were for a single car rollover with entrapment. The victim was still stuck inside.

I climbed in the Captain's seat, because I was not certified to drive at the time. The only other on-duty firefighter there had to drive. The two of us rushed toward the scene hoping volunteers would respond from home to give us a hand. Being that it was a weekday around four thirty in the afternoon, it was unlikely we would have much reinforcement.

We headed on the outskirts of town toward the state forest land to find a coupe rolled over on its top. The firefighter blocked the scene with our engine and told me to grab the trauma bag. He walked up to the scene to assess for injuries as I grabbed equipment.

My heart started pumping when I saw the scene. We had ourselves a real call with only the two of us to manage it. When we had adequate staffing, many times I would be placed in a supportive role such as traffic control. This time there would be no option other than throwing me right into the action. Whether I was ready or not, I was going to be doing it all.

As I started approaching the vehicle, I could see a person inside screaming in pain. My mind was overwhelmed with thoughts as I took everything in. Skid marks lined the pavement around the corner indicating the vehicle lost control and went off the roadway momentarily. The car flipped as it returned back to the pavement until it slid to a stop between both lanes of traffic. The driver was lying on the inside of the roof. I imagined he probably wasn't wearing a seatbelt from the way he had been thrown around.

The firefighter walks around the vehicle to check for any hazards. I approach from the driver side door and kneel down. I didn't know what to do. I was waiting for the ranking member to give me an order. The best I could do was talk to the man and reassure him that we would help him out.

"Hey, are you alright?" I ask awkwardly.

"Oh! Fuck! Oh, God! Help me! Help me!" the man screams. I felt helpless.

The firefighter returns and we try to move the victim from the wreckage but he won't budge. Initially hidden by his body, we find that the driver's arm is pinned underneath the vehicle through the sunroof opening.

"He's trapped underneath. Get the extrication equipment. Make sure you bring the ram!" I am told.

I get up immediately and start hauling off towards the engine. I was excited. We had a plan and I had a task to do. I was hoping I would be the one to get to operate the extrication equipment. I had never used the tools on a real scene before. Usually I was outranked for that task, which only made sense. The tools required technical skill and I did not have the experience to be messing around with them in a real situation. That was better left for training. The only problem was that training came far and few between. It was a common problem with our lack of funding.

As I approached the vehicle with equipment in hand, the voice from the trapped patient became clear again.

"Oh, God, get me out of here! Get me out of here! Oh, God!"

The man reeks of alcohol.

"Please, get me out of here!" he continued pleading.

My time in fire academy cutting open vehicles started coming back to me. I quickly noted the key points our instructors had drilled into our heads during training as I began hooking up the hydraulic lines and starting the portable compressor. I checked the function of the ram briefly and with the over watch of an experienced firefighter next to me, I began working on freeing the patient.

"Put the flat end of the ram on the pavement, right here." The firefighter points to a landmark. "Alright, find a solid piece of metal on the frame." He searches around the doorframe of the vehicle trying to find a sturdy point of contact that will hold during the lift. I try to stay focused on the task, centering my thoughts on the directions given while trying to drown out the screams coming from the frantic occupant.

"Here," he finds a solid piece. "Put the ram in there and lift." I follow direction.

"Go slowly..." he warns me. As the ram extends, the sound of crushing metal and plastics come from the piece of frame slowly wrapping itself around the hydraulic tool.

Finally, the car is done crumpling and a point of structural integrity is achieved causing the car to lift. Little by little we make progress. The car gets higher millimeters at a time. The screaming almost ceases as the weight of the vehicle gradually releases from the driver's arm.

"Slowly..." the firefighter re-affirms, almost as if something was about to go wrong.

Then, *SNAP!* The bottom of the ram slides out violently and the car comes crashing down to the pavement back onto man's arm.

"Oh, fuck! Ah, fuck!" the man screams!

"Shit!" I say quietly to the firefighter with a frantic look on my face. I'm panicking inside, but trying to hold my composure outwardly. *That should have never happened,* I thought to myself. *I must have placed it in the wrong position. I didn't set it on the pavement correctly before extending.* All sorts of destructive thoughts clouded my mind.

The firefighter hands the ram back to me and calmly gives direction. "Turn the ram around so the spike end is in the pavement this time and let's try that again."

That's not the right way to use it, I think. *That's not what how we were trained in academy. Although, it didn't work when we used it the correct way either.* With more apprehension this time, I give it another shot placing it exactly as I was told.

"Oh, God! I swear I will never do it again! I swear, God! I will never do it again!" the man screams.

The car begins lifting. The spike end of the ram digs into the pavement as more metal and plastic begin crunching. I let off briefly and assess.

"Keep going. You got this!" the firefighter reassures me.

I give it a bit more push.

"Come on. Keep going."

Finally, the car lifts from the pavement and the firefighter and I drag the patient out of the vehicle.

EMERGENCY MEDICAL TECHNICIAN

What's The Worst Thing You've Ever Seen

People think they have a grasp on what EMTs and Paramedics do in the streets, but much of that is from the portrayal we get in the media and movies. People would tell me how action-packed my job must be. How I have probably seen so many gruesome things. How I was such a hero for being willing to do what I do. I didn't feel like a hero. I wasn't one.

When I think of a hero, I think of a war veteran who fought for something much bigger: our freedom and security. Their sacrifice was much greater than what I was doing in the field. I could never understand it personally because I hadn't experienced what they'd been through. Those men and women deserved such a title. Not me.

My days were not action-packed. They were months of boredom followed by an isolated hour of nerve-racking unknowns known as a good call. Most weren't very gruesome visually. Emotionally they were. I wasn't scraping brains off the pavement after an accident on the highway. I wasn't stepping in pools of blood from a gunshot victim. Although their wounds were real, they were in a way anticlimactic. I thought the same way everyone else did before I got into this field. I thought it would be a rush to see. But, after seeing what was offered, I prayed each response would end up being a false alarm.

I packed those demons away. In public, I refrained from wearing any medical-type clothing to avoid the inevitable conversation. I didn't want recognition. I especially didn't want to talk to those who didn't understand it and had never experienced it. It was not every day that we were exposed to gruesome scenes, but it did happen and those memories stayed with you forever.

The dreaded question was brought up while I was getting my haircut at a small studio.

"So, what do you do?" the stylist asked.

"I work on an ambulance," I told her, knowing where this was leading. It always led there.

"You probably see some pretty crazy stuff, huh?" she followed.

I shrug it off. "Yeah, I don't know. There's always something interesting going on out there."

"Like, you've seen blood and guts and everything, right?" she pried further.

"It's not like the movies. It's not really like that. We just show up to people's houses and help them out with their problems."

"So, what's the worst thing you've ever seen?"

There it is. There is no avoiding it. But I try to divert anyways.

"I don't know. It's not really all that crazy, but it is fun and interesting and way better than a desk job," I tell her.

She keeps pushing the question, "Oh, come on, I'm sure you've seen something!"

I smile. "You know, there have been some pretty mangled vehicles from car wrecks and stuff."

"I'm going to school to be a nurse. Come on, I can handle it."
I sigh. *Fine,* I think.

"Have you ever seen a dead baby before?" She stops trimming and has a blank stare on her face. "Mother shoved a baby wipe down her own baby's throat because it wouldn't stop crying."

I look up in the mirror. Her face drops as she slowly starts speaking, "Oh, uh, I guess I didn't want to know..."

The rest of my haircut was peacefully quiet.

Don't Say Needles

Kids made me nervous. It wasn't until I had children of my own that I became more comfortable running calls on pediatric patients. I was uncomfortable because of my lack of experience interacting with the little guys. It was a whole new realm which changed the way I performed my entire assessment and interaction. The scenes provided so much more emotional attachment. They couldn't be thought of as subjects or quickly discarded as someone who did this to themselves. They were innocent little human beings who hadn't yet had the opportunity to fully live life.

   I had just been accepted into an emergency services program through a college in Oregon. I moved down south about two and a half hours away with my future wife, Sheila, to pursue an education that would help turn my passion into a career.

   I quickly got picked up as an EMT by an ambulance company operating in the city. I had gained confidence in my abilities as a volunteer, but now it felt different. It felt real. Through earning a paycheck, I felt as if I had a higher level of accountability for my actions. I wasn't just there helping out in my free time as a volunteer any longer. This was how I was going to make a living. The weight of responsibility was heavy.

I was immediately placed in a field training program. In academics, I excelled. But at nineteen, I had no idea how little the book would prepare me for real life. I was no longer going to be in the support role like I typically was as a volunteer. I would be directly involved in patient care and expected to perform to the expectations of my title.

I knew how to perform simple skills like taking a blood pressure or dressing a wound. With experience, I had become better at identifying sick patients. But I still did not know how to talk to people. It felt awkward being so young and questioning others much older than me about their conditions. It was uncomfortable for me to talk to an old woman about menopause or to talk to some young girl about her period. It was uncomfortable talking to anyone about their unhealthy behaviors which led to a chronic illness that I really did not fully understand.

Nervousness showed right through as I spoke to these people. I was never an outgoing person growing up so being put in a professional role where I was forced to be only made it worse. I was performing an assessment on a heavier set woman who was complaining of difficulty breathing. Without taking into consideration that she was actually breathing effortlessly and had no other symptoms, my mind told me I should rule out an allergic reaction. I blurted out, "Is your face more swollen today than normal?"

She responded, "Oh, honey, my face is always this fat."

Unfortunately, my communication skill didn't improve very quickly after that. Toward the end of my training, we were toned out for a motorcycle accident involving a young kid. He had landed wrong coming off a jump and hit his head. He was wearing his helmet and protective pads at the time of the accident, but was still looking dazed.

We secure the boy to a backboard and start heading off toward the hospital. "An easy code three," the training officer requests to the EMT driving. I go through the standard exam not even realizing that we were headed back to the hospital priority. There were no broken bones and no major bruising found. The helmet did a good job protecting his head, but he was slow to respond to our questions.

"Let's rule out a blood sugar issue before we get to the hospital," my preceptor hints at me. "Have you ever done one of those before?"

"No, we didn't do those where I was before."

"Okay, it's pretty easy." He continues to take me through the process.

I was going to have to poke the kid's finger with a small needle. Through my training, we were taught appropriate ways to talk with and examine pediatric patients. Working from the feet up during an exam helped build trust in your actions. Letting them touch some of the equipment before using it was another effective method to help them remain calm and cooperative. You were never supposed to lie to the patient. Instead, a better approach was to come up with a creative, non-fearful way of explaining the procedure. The one thing that stuck in my mind was my instructor telling our class, "Never use the word *needle* in front of kids."

I grabbed the glucometer. All I could think of was the word *needle*. I tried to come up with a better way to explain how I was going to poke the poor kid's finger without saying the dreaded word, but all I could think was *needle*. I couldn't stall any longer without my training officer getting on me.

Feeling the pressure, I finally made my move. "Um, uh... have you ever had a needle before?" I ask.

I cringed at the word that just came out of my mouth. *Needle? Why did I just say that?*

I could feel my trainer's judgment.

"No," the kid says calmly, with the same blank stare on his face. Maybe it was the trauma from his head injury keeping him calm. At least the pain was over for me. I poked the kid's finger and moved on with the rest of the call.

LITTLE SHITS

I would have never imagined where my life would have taken me after becoming an EMT. Although I had been exposed to a great deal of unpleasant events as a volunteer, nothing had prepared me for what I was about to experience. It was the pivotal shift which showed me the true colors of my career choice. It was one that would keep haunting me.

  I had just finished the field training program and had been cleared to work as an EMT alongside a Paramedic partner. I was three shifts in to my new schedule and was placed on an ambulance covering the east end of the city. I worked with an older and much more experienced paramedic. Although he was a bit disheveled, his medicine was solid.

  I always feared the older guys because I thought they would have less tolerance for rookie behaviors. I was nervous for most of the shift. Oddly, after our last call that night, my nerves went away. I think I finally experienced what I had feared. It took facing that fear head on to really move forward and gain comfort in my position. Unfortunately, once the fear and nervousness went away completely, all that was left was bitterness.

Twenty four hours was a long time to not make a mistake. I tried to stay sharp by using my free time to study medical books and familiarize myself with the city's layout.

I was beginning to enjoy my job. I just needed to get past the nervous phase and it would be more comfortable showing up to work. I figured I could get used to a career where I got paid to watch TV and sleep between running exciting calls.

That illusion quickly faded away the moment the tones went off. Immediately, the comfort was gone as my nerves kicked back in. The shift had gone smooth. I was so worried about making a mistake. I was hoping to have a quiet night and end the shift on a positive note in the eyes of my medic. Instead, I waited anxiously for the dispatch.

"Medic three. Respond on a pediatric respiratory arrest..."

"Oh, shit. That's not good," the medic says, getting off the couch faster than I have seen him move before.

We rush to the ambulance and I get in the driver's seat. I flip on the emergency lights and start heading to the end of our driveway.

"Where am I going?" I ask. I hated not knowing how to navigate the city without asking.

"Take a right on the main road, go to the stoplight, and take a left."

"Okay." My heart was racing.

"Go up to those apartments there on the right." he tells me. I drive up with the engine racing. "Slow down! Slow down! You're going to miss it! Turn right into the parking lot, right there."

I entered the apartment complex. Just ahead of us, the engine company calls on scene. As we push through the speed bumps in the parking lot we get a call from the Captain.

"Medic three, Engine eight, what's your ETA?"

My partner grabs the radio, "Were in the complex."

"Head straight down. We're at the end on your right."

I head to the back of the complex until I spot flashing lights. I barely come to a stop before my partner jumps out and sprints to the front door.

What am I supposed to do? I wonder. I didn't want to sit around indecisively. I was used to being given direction. *I guess now I need to be able to think on my own and take action without being told. That's what I was getting paid for.*

The only thing I could think to do was grab the gurney.

I hurry to the back of the ambulance, open the doors, and reach for the stretcher. Before I can even get a grip on the handle, the group of firefighters and my paramedic partner swarm the back doors of the rig.

"Get out of the way!" my partner shouts at me.

I quickly step aside. The firefighter closest to me is holding the baby. He is blue and lifeless. He looks to be about six months old.

"Get up front and drive!" I hear my medic shout. I frantically move out of the path and make my way to the front seat of the rig.

The firefighters hop in the back and set the baby's limp body on the gurney. I take a moment to look back in the compartment through the rearview mirror.

Everyone is moving fast and soon my view of the kid is obstructed. The Captain shouts, "Go! Go! Go! Drive!"

Heading out of the complex, I suddenly realized I had no idea which way to turn to get to the hospital. I looked back hoping someone would give me direction, but everyone was busy working the child. They had just started compressions. I couldn't think straight. I needed to make a decision.

Right or left? Fuck! Which way?

It was a fifty-fifty shot, but the consequences of a wrong decision were more than I could bear. If there was any chance the kid was going to make it, I needed to get my shit together and think.

My brain wasn't working. I knew the answer was in there, but hundreds of other thoughts scrambled any rational thinking at the moment. I decided to just go for it. I pushed the gas pedal and turned left. As soon as I started the turn, I hear, "Stop! Stop!" from the back.

I look back.

"It's a right! Turn right!" my partner shouts while he is working on the patient.

"You don't know how to get out of here?" the Captain in the airway seat asks, looking back at me.

"No," I respond. "Just get me back to the main road and I will know it from there."

"Alright, dude, turn right onto this road, get to the end of the street and take a left. That will get you back to the main road. You can get to the hospital from there right?"

"Yeah, yeah, thanks!" I respond quickly.

I get on the radio, "Dispatch, medic three transporting priority with one to Salem Hospital."

I was all sorts of flustered but in the moment I didn't even have enough time to feel my nerves. The call was not over yet and there was still room to screw up. It was a huge rush, but not the rush I was looking for. I thought running emergencies were going to be fun and exciting. This was not fun. There was nothing exciting about the situation. A child was dying in the back and every decision I made affected the outcome.

As I made my way closer to the hospital, police units in the area blocked approaching traffic with their vehicles to give us a clear path to our destination. It was amazing seeing a team of people in the city work together for one common purpose. With the hospital in sight, I look back at the patient. The medics inserted a breathing tube to attempt to oxygenate the child's body. It was almost over.

We pull into the ambulance bay and are met by a doctor and a few nurses. I grab the gurney and slowly wheel the patient out. A firefighter follows my movements while holding the tube in place. Another keeps pumping the chest. It doesn't look good.

The patient gets moved to the hospital bed and I leave with the gurney to start cleaning equipment. I get half way down the hall when a firefighter rushes out of the patient's room and runs towards me.

"Wait up," he yells. I stop. "Where is the baby wipe?"

I look at him puzzled. I have no idea what he is talking about. "I haven't seen any," I tell him. I assumed he was looking for something to clean equipment. I'd never had anyone ask for baby wipes before.

"The baby wipe was just here. It was right here on the gurney! Did you throw it away?" He is getting angry now. Another firefighter comes out to check.

"It's not here, check on the patient again. And check the trash. He might have thrown it away."

I stand defensively but quiet. I know I hadn't thrown anything away. The firefighter goes back into the room and I slowly start walking back to the ambulance bay. I hear the nurse talking to the firefighter from behind the curtain as I further my distance, but can't make out what she was saying.

"No, she shoved the fucking wipe..." the voice of the firefighter trails off as I round the corner and exit the building.

I decide not to touch anything until I was sure they had found what they were looking for. Instead, I waited in the bay for my partner to come out. I was glad the call was over. I was also dreading how the crew was going to respond to my performance.

My partner finally exits.

"What's with the baby wipe? Did they find it," I ask him quietly.

"Yeah they found it."

"Why was that so important?"

"The mom shoved the wipe down that kid's throat. It was so deep that we couldn't visualize it until we went in with the laryngoscope blade."

My heart sank. "Are you kidding me?"

"They were bagging him on scene but it was ineffective. I looked in the mouth a few times and didn't see anything. We found it when we went to tube him."

"She shoved a wipe down her baby's throat?" I respond with a look of disgust on my face. "Why would she do that?"

"Who knows? He probably wouldn't stop crying," he says. "She didn't even come out of her apartment when we grabbed the kid."

I just soaked it in and shook my head in disbelief.

Jesus!

As the firefighters walk out to the bay, the Captain pulls me aside.

"What's your name?"

This can't be good, I think, but I respond with, "Dave."

"Alright, Dave. I'm just going to say that this was a stressful call for everyone. But, we all have a job to do. You need to know your job and that includes driving, right?"

I shake my head in agreement.

"When we get a critical call, we rely on you knowing how to get around without direction. How long have you been working here?"

"This is my third shift," I tell him.

"Well, when we're in the back we have a job to do. We don't have time to think about it. We have to know our job inside and out. You have the same responsibility. Okay?"

"Alright," I shake my head, relieved the conversation was over.

We head back to the station.

It was one in the morning. I was wide awake, along with my partner. We sat on the couch again but this time without TV. The station was dark and quiet. Only light reflecting from the outside shined in as we reflected on the call mentally. Nothing else in the world was important at that moment. We weren't thinking about anything else, just the baby.

My partner breaks the silence.

"There was this one time we had this little shit that we kept giving him fluids and no matter what we did we couldn't get his blood pressure up..." His voice drifted off as background noise as my mind kept wandering back to the scene we just experienced. We didn't want to talk about it, but there was no avoiding it.

He continues, "When I was new, I had this other little shit that fell from an upstairs bedroom window. I guess the parents weren't watching him and he slipped right out, landed on his head..." He goes on as a way to release tension from the previous call. I guess any thought was better than the most recent. I just sat and listened as he reminisced about other *little shits* that filled his mind.

Right of Way

Months had passed since the baby incident. I refused to believe it had affected me. You had to have thick skin to make it in this business. I was becoming stronger in my skills and more confident in my abilities. I knew I had what it took to make it to the level of veteran medic. They had seen it all and moved past it. So would I. It was off my mind. Just a call from the past I could put in my experience bank. The more I added to it the better I would perform in the future.

Even through the rough periods, I was still fueled by the excitement of calls. I loved driving lights and sirens weaving in and out of traffic and running red lights. Now that I was living in Denver, I expected to see more crazy situations. I was amped up about the opportunity. I wanted the experience. Well, at least to a point. The volume of responses had definitely increased. My initial years of sitting at a station watching TV and getting sleep on duty appeared to be over.

My orientation rides in this new system proved we would be consistently pulling all-nighters. I was fine with that. The more patient contacts I could get before paramedic school the better. Plus, we usually had better calls at night and that's what I was there for.

It still felt odd getting excited over other people's pain and misery, but that feeling was starting to numb. It was boring sitting around waiting for something to happen. I needed some action to be able to prove my skill level. If it came at someone else's expense, that wasn't my problem. I couldn't stop bad things from happening to other people but I could mitigate the damage.

I was sitting backward in the airway seat in the back of the ambulance while we were responding on another consecutive call. The day had been packed full of great patient contacts. I turned my body as much as I could to keep an eye on the road ahead of us while we were forcing our way through traffic and clearing intersections. We were responding for abdominal pain at the north end of our district. Flu season brought a whole wave of 911 calls with people who had stomach cramping, fevers, and vomiting.

As we were inching forward through another intersection, I hear the sound of crushing plastic and screeching tires.

"Holy shit!" my partner yells. I leaned in further to get a better view and caught a glimpse of a man being tossed through the air. He lands on the pavement just beyond the crosswalk in the middle of the intersection. Our driver moves up a bit to block traffic in our new work zone.

"Did you see that?" my partner yells at me in excitement. "He flew like ten feet in the air!"

He grabs the radio, "Dispatch, Medic 102, put us on an auto versus motorcycle. One patient, send fire. Also send a unit to replace us on our original call."

The medic who had been training me approached the downed man and I follow closely behind her. The man was on the ground and still awake. After checking for injuries, I headed back to the rig to grab a backboard. I figured I should have brought one to the patient initially, but the excitement from the incident had me distracted at that point. I guess I still had some little quirks to work out but at least I was noticing them now and improving myself daily.

As I walked back, the driver who hit the motorcyclist stepped out of her van. She was still on her cell phone as she approached us.

"Hey! He just stopped in front of me all of a sudden," she says.

"Yeah, because we were going through the intersection," the medic yells at her. "We were trying to respond on another call."

"I didn't see you guys. You weren't even in the intersection yet and he slammed on his brakes!" Her demeanor insisted she did nothing wrong.

"You didn't see us or hear us because you were too busy talking on your phone." My medic looks at the motorcyclist still lying on the ground. "He did the right thing and came to a stop to let us through."

I try to ignore the pissing match and bring equipment to the patient's side. From there my EMT partner and I work the patient.

The woman, with the cell phone still up to her ear, starts walking back towards her van. She gets in the driver's seat and puts the vehicle in reverse.

My medic halts and once again has to direct her attention away from the patient. She marches over pointing her arm at the woman.

In an authoritative voice, she yells, "Stop!"

The woman stops and pokes her head out the rolled down window but doesn't say anything.

"Don't even think about moving that van, you stay right there!" she orders.

The EMT gets on his portable and tells dispatch, "Can you send police to our location?"

The woman's reply is muffled by the street noise. My attention keeps shifting from the patient to the scene around me.

45

"No, I saw you!" the medic yells. "You were on your phone. You're not going anywhere."

"Let's get him out of the street," the EMT tells me. We roll the patient onto the backboard and load him into the back of the rig. Eventually the medic returns.

"You guys need anything back there?" she asks us. Normally, she rode in the back with me. We had patients who were nowhere near as critical earlier and she always rode backwards, keeping a close eye on me. I just stared at her as those thoughts raced through my head. *Was she still pissed at the other lady and just wanted to drive? Maybe she trusted me enough at this point to let me be free in the back with the other EMT.*

"Yeah, we're good back here," my partner responds.

We start heading off toward the hospital. With a large bore IV in hand, while bouncing down the rough Aurora streets, I insert the needle into the motorcyclist's arm and hang a bag of fluids. I had come a long way from a system where we weren't even allowed to check a patient's blood sugar. This is what the job was all about and I loved every moment of it!

Falling Off a Cliff

My life changed forever hours before Cinco de Mayo of 2009. I had just finished my Paramedic training when I first became a father. I couldn't be any happier after seeing my baby boy for the first time. Our little family was growing and I couldn't wait to see what life had in store for Sheila and me.

I felt I had an advantage in fatherhood being a medic because I was comfortable managing emergencies. I knew what to do if there was an injury or something worse. The curse was that I also remembered every accident I had responded to involving children. I had seen kids who had been hit by cars. I had seen those who have choked. I had seen them get their fingers cut off from the backs of doors. I constantly worried I would fail to protect my own son.

A father had been playing with his five year old son in the driveway after celebrating their favorite team's recent victory. The kid sat on his dad's shoulders before a simple turn of fate turned their life upside down. Although this event happened before I had children, the memory would stay with me throughout fatherhood.

We got called out for a possible head injury after a fall. We arrived at the house and found a kid being cradled by his parents. He was crying a bit and had blood slowly oozing from the back of his head.

My medic partner dressed his wound while I checked a heart rate and blood pressure. As an EMT, this was a standard first step for me to take. The vitals were unremarkable. The kid appeared a little tired, but was answering our questions appropriately. I asked him what he was doing before the fall and he said, "Watching football with my dad." I asked him who won. With a smile on his face, he says, "The Broncos."

The fire department's medic finishes his assessment and tells us, "Well, everything is checking out. Unless I'm missing something, I think you guys can handle this."

There was something about this situation that didn't sit right. I had a gut feeling something was wrong. That little voice in the back of my head kept telling me to keep looking.

The kid was tired, but that was expected after a fall. There was nothing alarming about that. He still didn't look right, though. I pushed down on his nail bed to check how long it took his blood to refill the distil capillaries. The way the vitals presented, I expected instantaneous refill in color. Instead, his nail beds remained pale for an extended period.

"He's got a five second cap refill," I tell the medic. Judging from the lack of response, it felt as if I was the only one concerned. Kids have a tendency to compensate extremely well before they crash. When they decompensate, they go down hard.

The fire medic checked my result.

"Well, do you feel like you need another hand back there. We would be more than happy to ride with you."

I try to play off the fact that I could handle the call myself, but they decided to ride with me anyways. I guess my attempt to display confidence failed. They saw right through it and decided to ride with me anyways. Although they did not upgrade the call, which meant I got to maintain patient care at my certification level. We headed to the closest hospital routine, with no emergency signals.

"Do you want me to start a line?" I ask the medic.

"No, let's hold off on that for right now," he says, so I do as I am told.

During the transport, the kid becomes more and more tired. He begins closing his eyes for longer periods of time. Eventually, he only wakes up when stimulated with light pain.

"Are you getting tired?" I ask him.

"Uh huh," the five year old responds while trying to shake his head but unable to due to the cervical collar in place.

The kid quickly drifts back out.

I look at the medic and tell him, "He's out again."

The medic trades me spots and starts a neurologic exam.

"Hey, buddy. Wake up." He taps on his chest a couple times.

The kid opens his eyes but looks lethargic.

"Squeeze my hands," the medic tells him.

"Come on, squeeze my hands. There you go. No, more on the left side. Squeeze my left hand. Harder. No, the left hand. Squeeze my left hand..."

The medic moves down to checking the legs. "Push down with your feet like you're driving a racecar."

The kid tries to push.

"Move your left foot. Push down with your left foot. Push..."

The anticipation is killing me. It is obvious something is wrong. Most likely pressure is building up in the kid's head as a result of the trauma, crushing his brain. I did not want to step on the medic's toes, but I couldn't wait any longer for direction. I needed to take action. I finally made a move by grabbing an oxygen mask and placing it over the patient's face.

"How about an IV now?" I suggest.

"Get me the IV tray!" the medic responds. "And step it up priority," he shouts to my medic driving the ambulance.

I hand him the tray and work on spiking an IV bag. We work judiciously to get the necessary interventions performed before arriving at the hospital.

The medic calls the emergency department with an update on the patient's condition. We roll in and are directed to their major trauma room. As we wheel the unresponsive patient through the hallway, we are met by the nursing staff. One nurse asks, "Are you doing that with his arm?"

"Doing what?" I ask, wondering why she would be asking such a strange question. I look down and notice the kid's right arm has begun jerking.

"He's seizing! Get him on the bed!" the nurse directs her staff.

Almost every member of the emergency department entered the room to give a hand. Unfortunately, this particular hospital was underequipped to handle such a seriously sick child. They had to request airlift to a children's hospital and by the time we left, the helicopter had already taken off with the kid.

Life can change in an instant. There were many calls I would follow up on, but this one in particular I never pursued. Part of me didn't want to know if he had lived or died. I didn't want that to be with me forever. I wanted a happy ending to my story and the only for sure way to get that was to create it.

Once I had a baby of my own, my feelings toward calls involving children intensified. There was a mother who forced her child on a hot burner causing a perfect stovetop element burn mark on the toddler's rear end. There was a father who became enraged and pushed his infant and adolescent children down a flight of stairs. There was the boy who was punched in the stomach by his father so hard it caused internal bleeding. And of course, there was the woman who shoved a baby wipe down her baby's throat because it wouldn't stop crying.

There was no making sense of it. When my son was a month old, Sheila and I came to realize he had colic. There was nothing we could do to sooth him. I would sit with him lying in my arms for hours trying to comfort him but nothing worked. As I sat there, the images of those traumatized by their protectors haunted me.

I remembered the infant's lifeless body lying on the gurney and wondered if he had colic too. I wondered if his parents loved him at one point and just lost control. After hours of constant crying, I began praying for it to stop. I didn't know what to do. I didn't want to lose control. A public service for 'Don't shake a baby' came across the television. I looked at my child and smiled. Giving my son a tight hug, I thought, *I would never do that to you.*

Your Call, Buddy

As the years passed, I was settling nicely into my role as an EMT. I was becoming sure of myself, although I hadn't realized my full potential at the time. It took a lot less thinking on average calls for me to handle them fluently. I was also finding points in patient care where I would hit a barrier. There were injuries and illnesses that I had the knowledge and confidence to manage, but not the certification. If I wanted to advance in my career, it was time to start looking into a Paramedic program.

   I pushed to make a presence on scene. If the medic was interviewing a patient, I would question family members to uncover additional details. I stayed a step ahead of the medic by having equipment prepped before they asked for it. I already knew what the next step was. I felt a strong push to step in and help but there were limits put on me by my scope of practice.

I had the urge to advance my career, but at the same time I enjoyed feeling comfortable in my current position. The moment I was finally swayed to further my scope of practice occurred on what started out to be the most mundane call.

We responded to a street corner for a man in his fifties who was feeling sick and wanted a ride to the hospital. The man was well groomed, which I found odd. Most of our clientele on the streets were homeless or mentally ill. This man was neither. He sat there patiently awaiting our arrival in clean clothes while holding a small bag.

My medic began to interview the patient. After a brief assessment, he decides to hand the call off to me.

"He's complaining of dizziness. We can hook him up to the monitor in the back but otherwise he's okay to go routine."

The man stepped into the back of the rig and sat on our gurney. I hooked him up the EKG monitor and took a set of vitals. A brief, nonchalant conversation revealed something was off about this guy. He was a little slow to answer questions and was more focused on us leaving than assessing him. I wasn't about to get pushed to make a transport decision that quick without exhausting all of my options for acquiring information, so I question him further.

"So, what's going on? Why did you call 911 today?" I pressed, this time starting from the beginning.

"I haven't been feeling good. I've been dizzy and lightheaded," he answers slowly.

"How long has this been going on?" I ask.

"A couple hours now I guess."

"What are you doing out on a street corner?" I ask him. "Where do you live?"

He thinks for a minute before answering. "Down the block," he says, pointing into the neighborhood.

"Why are you all the way out here then?"

"I, uh, I didn't want my family to know I was calling 911."

My partner stays at the back of the rig listening.

"Why wouldn't you want your family to know?" I wondered. I maintain eye contact with him until he answers my question. I felt like I was on to something. I just didn't know what.

"I don't know. I didn't want them worrying about me."

"Which house is yours? Can you point to it?"

"It's the green one on the right," he tells me.

"Stone, what do you say we go down there and talk to them," my partner suggests. He gets up front and takes us further down the block until we reach the green house.

Family members emerge from the yard, frantically looking for their loved one. After spotting us, they immediately approach the ambulance. The wife opens the back doors, relieved to have found her husband.

"What are you doing in an ambulance, honey?" she asks. "We were looking all over for you! What's going on?"

"We're still trying to figure that out, ma'am," I interrupt the patient's attempt to sugarcoat the situation. "Are you his wife?"

"Yes," she says.

"Your husband doesn't seem right to me. He seems a little off. Is there anything that could be going on? Drugs or alcohol? New medication?"

"Oh no, he doesn't drink," she insists. "And he hasn't seen a doctor for quite a while."

"Has he been sick recently or had any car accidents or anything?"

"Well, he did fall a couple days ago when he was working on the garage."

My ears perk up. *I finally got something!*

"How far did he fall?"

"He was at the top of a ladder so probably ten feet or so."

"He fell ten feet? Did he lose consciousness?"

"He said he woke up on the ground. He had a huge lump on the back of his head."

"What did he land on?" I ask? "Pavement or dirt?"
"It's concrete."
"Okay, did he get seen afterward? Did you take him to the emergency room?"
"He insisted he was fine," she says. "He wouldn't let me take him to the hospital or even call 911."
"Well, that probably has something to do with what is going on today," I tell her.
The severity of the call had now been uncovered. I look at my medic partner and ask, "Are you taking this?"
"No. You figured it all out. This is your call, buddy!" he tells me.
I feel exhilarated to be given the opportunity to attend the call by myself! Allowing me to maintain care of the patient after discovering such a huge piece of the puzzle only demonstrated his confidence in me. If a medic didn't trust you, they wouldn't even let you talk to a patient. You would be told to get up front and drive.
I had finally accomplished what I was trying to achieve as an EMT. In this field, people talk to everyone. If you make one mistake, the entire system knows about it. I wanted people to talk about me in a good way. I was the EMT who discovered a critical issue no one else was able to find.
The most difficult patients were those in the grey area between obviously sick and not sick. Seriously sick patients typically required a treatment plan down a standard algorithm. Patients who were not sick only required a focused exam and possibly a ride to the hospital. Distinguishing a seemingly not sick patient and determining the true nature of their illness is what made a great medic. It was a skill which could not be taught. It could only be achieved through a determination to truly want to help people.

Reassurance

Near the end of my time as an EMT, I had the opportunity to work with one of the oldest and most knowledgeable paramedics in Colorado. He was in his sixties and had been in the field longer than I had been alive. He had an incredible knowledge base and an easy-going personality which made him pleasant to work with and easy to learn from.

There were a lot of egos in emergency services. Mainly, because the system was packed with type-A personalities who knew how to get the job done, but not necessarily how to get along with others. Sometimes those personalities clashed, but for the most part people figured out how to work together.

I was not type-A. As I thought about becoming a medic, I considered my ability to manage an emergency scene. In my personal life, I was quiet and did not like being in charge. I would rather make life easy by going with the flow. It felt different when I came to work. I had to be different. But, I was backed by the power the position created. I was an authority figure in the medical world, at least on the streets, and that gave me the confidence to push past my fears and step outside my boundaries. It was a necessary move if I wanted to be a successful paramedic.

Gaining the role meant even more power. I wanted to be the best I could and that meant my personality needed to change. It felt simple at the time. I had worked with some great personalities and some horrible ones. I knew I didn't want to develop into a self-centered asshole like many medics I had worked with. I was not going to let my ego get in the way. When I became a paramedic, I was going to work as a team with my EMT and respect them as a valuable asset.

The monotony of our day was broken with a call for an infant who had stopped breathing in a near-by apartment complex. I didn't have any kids at the time, and I had never really held a baby before. Unfortunately, my only experiences with children were the sick ones we kept seeing on the ambulance.

Instantly, my nerves shot through the roof as I recalled past events. I didn't have much time to quiet them down before we reached the scene. We pulled into the dark parking lot to find a young woman holding something in her arms and approaching the ambulance fast. She looked terrified. She kept approaching and all I could see were blankets in her arms. We roll to a stop and I reach for the door handle just as she approaches my side. I open the door and the woman frantically shoves the baby in my arms. There was no time to think.

"He's not breathing!" she screams. I start opening the load of blanket she had covering her baby.

Deep inside, I felt my stomach drop. But, the severity of the situation and my responsibility to act had me holding my composure. I kept digging in further to uncover the mess of blankets.

Finally, the face is revealed. The baby looks healthy. He is breathing and has a healthy pink skin color. I remove the blanket completely and gain a firm grip cradling the child. He has good muscle tone throughout his body. I put my finger in close and he grabs it with his tiny hand.

Just then, the medic had finally made his way around the front of the rig to get his eyes on the patient.

"He's awake, pink, breathing is fine, he has good muscle tone..." I say out loud, confirming to my partner what I had seen so far.

I ask the mom, "He's breathing now. Did he stop breathing at some point?"

"Yes, for two minutes!" she says, still hysterical. "He turned blue!"

"Was he choking on anything or did he just stop breathing?"

"No, he just stopped breathing!"

"An ALTE," my partner says quietly to me. I didn't know what he was talking about at the time.

"We will get him checked out at the hospital. He looks like he's doing fine now, okay," I reassure the mom.

I hand the phone over to my medic, expecting it to be his patient. He hands it back saying, "No, it's yours if you want it."

There was no question in my mind. I took the call.

Afterward, my partner pulled me to the side congratulating me on staying calm in a tense situation. He told me that I held my composure well and did an exceptional job assessing the situation.

"Most EMT's, and even some medics, freak out when they are given babies. You handled this one exceptionally well. You weren't afraid to step in and did a great job assessing him."

It's not often you get praise in this industry. For the most part, it is a thankless job, but when praise is given it is usually well deserved.

He finishes the conversation by saying, "You're going to make an excellent medic someday."

His words stuck with me. I was ready.

PARAMEDIC SCHOOL

No Crying on the Ambulance

Paramedic school was both the easiest and most difficult program I had to overcome. I excelled effortlessly through the didactic portion without any worries.

Our midterm was the toughest exam in the program. It had a history of producing the highest fail rate amongst students. The day of the exam, our instructor handed us the test booklet and invited us to meet him at a local bar after he had graded the exams. We were going to need stress relief either way after this grueling portion of the program.

I felt the pressure, but was not as nervous as most the other students. Failing this exam meant you failed the program. Judging from my performance so far, I had no worries about continuing through. The test was written in a way that you could not cram knowledge ahead of time to try and skate by. You really had to know the material inside and out.

At the end of the exam, I handed in my packet with confidence. A line of students gathered near the instructor, anxiously waiting for their tests to be graded. I skipped to the front of the line, handed the instructor my booklet, and headed straight to the bar.

A few classmates had finished the test before me and were already kicking back beers.

"How did you do? Did you pass?" they asked. "What score did you get?"

"I don't know?" I shouted to them as I ordered an IPA from the counter. "I didn't stay. So hopefully I passed."

"Oh, man, I couldn't handle not knowing."

"So you guys did well?" I asked.

"Yeah, we've all passed so far," they said with relief.

Within the hour, the instructor showed up and bought a round of beers for everyone.

I approached him. "Hey, how did I do?"

"I don't know what score you got, but I know you didn't fail," he yelled over the loud background noise. I smile and continue drinking. "Good job, man!"

The clinical portion didn't go so smooth.

My first shift on the medic unit was intimidating. I was being introduced to the old 'knife and gun club.' These medics were the best in the area and competed with the ranks of top EMS systems around the country. I was expected to know my shit inside and out. Now was my time to prove it by putting it into practical use. Every day was a test on the streets but the subject was always unknown. Anything could happen and I could either buck up and handle it or quit.

I blasted the most hardcore music on my drive to the downtown ambulance garage, screaming the lyrics at the top of my lungs to release any apprehension. Today I was going to be in the spotlight. Now the accountability was completely on me. I never experienced such a magnitude of responsibility before, but I was preparing myself mentally. This was my time to prove myself. Inside, I was ready for whatever the city threw at me.

I made my way into the bay and introduced myself to the preceptor who would be training me. I extended my hand out and we shook.

"Hi, so you're my student today?" he responded.

"Yes."

"Okay. Go check the rig out. I'll meet you in a minute and go over the equipment with you before we head out."

I opened the rig and took in the new surroundings. Things were situated differently than I was used to, so I started familiarizing myself with the layout. Minutes later, my preceptor interrupted the rig check to have a word with me in the back of the unit.

"How's everything looking?" he asks.

"Good so far. I still have to check the kits."

"I'm going to tell you what I tell everyone else on their first day here." I listen, intrigued about what I was about to learn. "You're a medic now so you're in charge today. I'm going to be hands off so don't kill anyone. If I think you're about to do something stupid I will step in, but I won't be very happy about it."

"Okay," I respond hesitantly. *What does he think I am going to do?*

"Also, there is no crying on the ambulance."

I raise my eyebrows at him in question with a bit of a smirk on my face.

He responds, "Oh, you think that's never happened? I've had grown men crying in front of me because things were too tough for them. Don't do anything stupid and I won't have to chew your ass out. If you want to cry, hold it in until the end of shift or go home early. There is no crying on the ambulance."

"I can take feedback so you won't have to worry about that," I say, nervously. The preceptor stands up and walks out of the rig.

"Finish your rig check," he yells back at me. "We're leaving in five minutes."

I take a deep breath. *Well, today's going to be interesting.*

In my head, I began reciting the subjects which made me nervous. I wondered what calls we would see today. I had ten hours ahead of me. What if I screwed up? I quickly silenced any negative self-talk and tried to imagine myself succeeding. I imagined my preceptor being proud of me, just like my previous medic partners had. There was nothing to worry about. I was ready for anything.

We get in service and are immediately dispatched on a call.

"Respond to Bannock and Colfax for an MVA with fire," the radio blares.

My preceptor calmly responds, "En route."

Holy shit! I think. *A car accident with a fire involved! This is going to be crazy.* I knew inner-city medicine was going to be pretty intense. The excitement from the scene I had created in my head was quickly overcome with the responsibility I now had to manage it. *I am the medic now. I'm in charge.*

I began going over treatment plans in my head. *It sounds like a pretty bad accident so I will want to have the patient on a backboard. If they are burned I will need to establish an IV and give fluids. Make it two IVs. Also we will need to cut off any smoldering clothing and cool the burns. And... Shit.* I start getting overwhelmed. *Okay, start with the basics: ABC's. Airway: they might need to be intubated if they have facial burns. Breathing: I will definitely want them on oxygen and I might need to breath for them. Circulation: I will need to check a pulse right away...*

We continue racing through traffic, swerving to get around stopped vehicles in front of us and slamming on our breaks at intersections to avoid cross traffic. As we approach, my preceptor calls, "On scene."

I turn my head around to peek out the front window at the situation we were approaching. There was no smoke. There were just a couple of cars in the intersection with the occupants walking around checking for damage. It was a fender bender. We spoke to the occupants quickly and everyone denied injuries. We clear the call with no patients.

As soon as we clear, we get tapped out on another one. Dispatch calls out, "Respond to the area of 16th and Market for an altered male with fire."

With fire? I wonder. It finally started making sense. *It must be the way they dispatch units in this city. Obviously the man is not on fire. They are sending the fire department along with our unit.*

We head out dodging traffic until we reach downtown. We arrive to the scene to find a drunk male sitting against a building on a major walkway.

"This is all you," my preceptor reminds me.

I approach the man head on.

"Move over. Watch your angle on him," I get told.

I move slightly to my left to get more advantage with my positioning. We were taught in class the basics of scene safety but it was something I always seemed to overlook.

Being eager to help, I start off with, "Hi, I'm Dave. I'm a paramedic here to check you out. What's going on today?"

"Fuck you," he mutters.

"Okay." I take a small step back and get down on one knee. My train of thought was instantly derailed, but I try to recover. "Is anything hurting? Anything wrong?" I question him. I reach in to check a pulse on his wrist but he pulls away. He looks as if I had just threatened him.

"Watch it, Stone," my preceptor warns after noticing the man's agitation.

"Leave me the fuck alone!" he slowly mumbles. I look back at my preceptor confused. *What do I do now?*

My preceptor steps in. "How much have you had to drink today?"

"Fuck you."

My preceptor looks at me. "Stone, you're going to need to check his head, chest and back for trauma and get a D-stick. You don't know if he's a diabetic, head injury, or what. If he's clear, he's going to detox."

This wasn't going as smooth as I imagined my first patient contact proceeding as a paramedic student. I didn't want my preceptor stepping in. I wanted to do the exam and make a transport decision. I had done it many times as an EMT with no problem. But now, I just wanted this call to be over.

People had always been open to me assessing them and providing treatment. This guy didn't want me anywhere near him. He just wanted to be left alone. He wasn't hurting anyone. He was drunk in public. It seemed like a police matter. But, my preceptor was right. There could be any number of things wrong with him and since we were called out, we needed to assess him. He had no legal right to refuse treatment because he was altered mentally. I had to operate with the understanding that he would accept help in a reasonable state of mind.

The man had a hat and bandana covering his head and a thick jacket covering his body. I timidly worked my way toward removing his clothing.

"Alright, sir, I am going to have to take off your hat so I can check out your head really quick..."

"You're not touching my fucking hat!" he snaps at me, grabbing at my arm.

My preceptor lurches forward at him, stopping the advance. My arm is released.

"Hey, asshole!" my preceptor shouts at the man. This gets his attention. He slowly turns his body toward the new voice. "You want to talk like that to me, that's fine, but you're not going to talk to my student like that!"

The man clenches his fists and tenses up his body. On his face is pure hatred. His buzz is overcome with adrenalin. He is ready to fight.

The man makes his move toward me again. Before he can get in a position to cause any harm, my preceptor grabs him by the back of the head and forces his entire body down on the pavement.

"Check him, Stone!" he shouts. I step back in and remove the man's hat and bandana. I swipe my gloved hands across all sides of his head and find no blood or injuries. I pull the man's jacket up as far as possible and swipe around his back and chest. Again, I find nothing. I poke his finger and sample his blood sugar, which comes back normal.

My preceptor lets go of the man. He sets himself back in a seated position against the building and brushes off the dirt and debris from his face.

"You guys are assholes!" he mutters.

He's going to detox.

Inner-city medicine was far different than what I was used to. I grew up in a system where patients looked forward to me helping them. It was something I was going to have to get used to in order to survive the program.

The day never lost pace. As nighttime set and the final hours of my first shift ticked away, we got called out for one more response. Our unit arrived to a night club where we found a young female unconscious at the doorway. The woman was alone with a crowd of spectators encircling her, but keeping their distance at the same time. We broke through the crowd and I started my assessment. She didn't wake up to pain but was still breaking. I asked the crowd if anyone knew what happened, but only got shrugs. My preceptor walks up with the gurney and we load the girl in the back of the rig. There is no time wasted. Immediately, we speed off toward the hospital priority.

My preceptor tells me, "If you want to do something advanced and you have been trained, go ahead and do it. Otherwise, tell me what you need and I will do it for you." We had been trained in many advanced skills to that point in the program, but there were still others we hadn't been cleared to perform in the field. It was an awkward stage in training where you were expected to perform like a medic but still felt like an EMT.

I start by hooking up the blood pressure cuff.

"What are you doing?" my preceptor questions.

"Getting a set of vitals," I respond, tightening the device around the patient's limp arm. I was working more off of habit than actually thinking through the situation.

"No, you're not a God damn basic anymore!" he shouts. "Treat your patient. What is the first thing you should be doing?"

"Airway," I say.

"What do you need to do with the airway?" he keeps pushing me along.

"I checked it. It's open and she is breathing."

My preceptor pulls out a nasopharyngeal tube which functions by holding the tongue back from obstructing a path for breathing in an unconscious patient.

"Have you ever put one of these in before?"

I hesitate for a second, not wanting to admit my lack of skill, but eventually respond, "No, I haven't."

My preceptor lubes the patient's nose and instructs me on its placement. "Insert it straight down, just like this," he says as he inserts the small tube into the patient's right nare. He immediately pulls it out. "Now, you do it."

I switch seats with the preceptor and instinctively try to place the device at the wrong angle and my preceptor corrects me. "No, straight down and give it a twist when you meet resistance."

By now the NPA is a bit bloody from repeated use. This time, I insert it the correct way and place an oxygen mask on the girl.

"What else do you want to do?" he asks.

"IV."

"Get on it then." I grab my equipment and move to position myself at the proper angle for insertion.

"Can you spike me a bag?" I ask.

"When you're signed off you are going to have to do all of this on your own. There won't be anyone else back here helping you so you need to figure it out," he says tossing an IV bag to me. I rope off the girl's arm and attempt to insert a needle into the largest vein I can find. I felt the pressure of the situation which was only intensified by my preceptor.

I missed the first attempt. I look to the bench seat for a small dressing to stop the bleeding but couldn't find one. I had prepared for the insertion, but not for a miss.

"Can you get me a four by four?" I ask my preceptor.

"You need to figure this out, Stone. You're back here by yourself."

God damnit! I search frantically for something to control the bleeding but I can't find anything within reach.

"You better have an IV in before we arrive," he continues to antagonize me. He wants me to feel the pressure. He wants to see how I think and how I operate when things are going wrong. He wants to see if I will break mentally. I am beyond flustered at this point, but I try to stay focused. The problem is not going away. I still have a patient to help.

Fuck it! I figure. The blood was only dribbling out from the missed stick so I let her arm flop by her side. I grab another IV needle and attempt on the opposite arm. I dig around without any luck finding a vein until the back doors of the rig open up.

"We're here, buddy. Time to go," the driver tells me.

We unload the patient and I walk into the emergency room defeated. As we roll through, a trail of blood dripping from each dangling arm follows us. I want to hide as I hear distant laughs from the nursing staff.

As the shift came to an end, my preceptor began filling out paperwork that would be turned in to the program directors. We reviewed his remarks together.

"Alright, I like to start with the positives from the day before we get into areas where you can improve. So to start with a positive, you showed up today and you showed up on time."

He pauses and looks at me for a second before continuing.

"That was good. And you were in uniform. We always appreciate that. Ok, now for the negatives..."

I brace for it.

"Hey, I'm just messing with you!" he says laughing a bit. "No, you did fine today. Pretty average for the first day, actually. You need to be more assertive and get yourself in there. But as far as working under pressure and determining sick versus not sick, I think you did fine. So, do you have any questions for me?"

"No, I just wanted to say that I did learn a lot. I think I learned more here in one day than I have working as an EMT," I say.

"Good. That's what we want to hear."

I took my paperwork, strung my backpack across my back, and walked out of the garage to my car. I was glad the shift was over. I was glad I hadn't screwed up too badly, but I knew I had to step it up next shift. I needed to be assertive. I needed to be a leader.

But, hey, at least I didn't cry on the ambulance.

Invisible Boy

I didn't know how to be a leader. In my head, I could imagine myself walking into a scene and managing it flawlessly. I could delegate tasks and think calmly under pressure. Real life was far different. I wasn't living up to the image I had created for myself.

I still did not feel like a paramedic. I knew enough to be dangerous but lacked the experience to be proficient. There was a great deal of apprehension holding me back. I knew what my role was supposed to entail, but I didn't feel that I was there yet. Confidence would come with experience, but my lack of it held me back from performing to my full capability.

We were assigned shifts with a variety of preceptors. It was both a good thing and a bad thing. I enjoyed working with different paramedics because of their various levels of experience and unique ways of teaching. It gave students an advantage to learn the same job from an array of sources. On the other hand, it felt as if you were always starting from square one. Each shift entailed earning respect and confidence and learning to work with yet another personality.

I was always nervous to meet my next preceptor. One in particular had a reputation of having an irrational hatred toward students. Still early in my internship, I walked anxiously into the office to introduce myself to this woman.

As it turned out, the image others created of her was completely wrong. She was welcoming while introducing herself and seemed energetic about instructing me. After working a shift together, I found her to be a great preceptor. She had the patience to sit back and allow me to progress through a call without jumping in and passing judgment early. I needed that. My approach was unorganized which made most of my preceptors assume I didn't know what I was doing.

It was obvious I had difficulty managing scenes. While examining patients, I felt the pressure of my preceptors watching every move I made. As I progressed through calls, I imagined them criticizing every choice I made. Regardless, this preceptor maintained a positive attitude and put all her effort in towards pushing me past my fears.

We had a call for a younger female who attempted suicide. She was eight months pregnant and going through a recent breakup with her boyfriend. Guilt and depression from these events caused her to want to take her life by consuming a handful of pills.

The girl was still awake and talking with us. Under the eyes of my preceptor, I gained a minimal amount of information on scene and worked to move the patient to our medic unit.

My preceptor stayed outside of the patient compartment for a few minutes to chat with the firefighters. From her perspective, there were still a lot of unanswered questions. But, while she was outside talking, I took the opportunity to gather the rest of the story from the patient. I felt comfortable being by myself. It felt as it had when I was an EMT. I no longer had fear of doing the wrong thing. I wouldn't be criticized. I couldn't hurt the patient by asking questions.

I could only embarrass myself. But without witness, that wasn't going to happen. The pressure of constantly being tested was temporarily relieved and I allowed myself to finally relax and think clearly.

My preceptor entered the rig as I was starting an IV. She sat down near the patient's head and started asking the same questions I had just asked, assuming I had gotten nowhere further in my assessment.

"How far along are you?"

I answer for the patient. "She is thirty-two weeks pregnant and is getting prenatal care. She has had an ultrasound with no problems. This is her first pregnancy. She broke up from her boyfriend recently and has been feeling depressed. She told me she took a handful of Xanax over an hour ago but didn't know how many. I'm going to give her an IV."

My preceptor had a surprised look on her face.

"Well then, okay. Wow. You got a lot done when I was outside." I felt a sense of comfort after seeing the praised look on her face. She had faith in me. I just needed to show what I was capable of.

After the call, my preceptor began telling me a story.

"Have you seen the movie Mystery Men?"

"No," I answer. I had never heard of the movie.

"Well, in the movie there is a superhero called Invisible boy whose super power is that he can turn invisible, but only when no one is looking."

"Well, that's not very effective is it," I respond chuckling, not exactly sure what she was getting at.

"I think that's you. You're invisible boy."

It started to make sense. When I had the pressure of preceptors watching my every move, I began getting nervous and apprehensive about my decisions. I would get flustered with details of the patient and the call would go downhill from there. I was focusing on my fears and not on the patient. I was afraid of failing. I was afraid of being ridiculed. I imagined them criticizing every choice I made which only caused me to second guess every decision. On the other hand, when no one was watching I was able to effectively perform my job. She knew I had the knowledge and ability to be a great paramedic. I just needed to overcome the mental barrier that was holding me back.

I didn't want to be invisible boy. It wasn't the first time I had felt that way, though. The subject was just out in the open now. I knew what I needed to do now to improve but for some reason my mind wouldn't allow me. It was a barrier I wasn't sure I could push past. Before my next shift started, I arrived early to the education department and sat down in the program director's office. I had no intention of boarding the medic unit that day.

"So, what's going on Dave? How have your rides been going?" he asks.

"That's what I wanted to talk to you about." I take a deep breath.

I had never experienced defeat before. After reviewing how I had actually performed, I was unsure how I was going to continue through the program. "I am not really sure I'm meeting the standards of the program. I thought I was ready to get on the medic unit but I'm really struggling with the role of being in charge and making decisions. I've kept reading through the book to learn more but it's not helping. I just..."

I pause for a second and think through what I am about to say.

"I think maybe I don't have enough experience and that I need to work as an EMT for one more year and then come back."

It was tough getting it out, but deep down it was how I truly felt. As the words flowed from my mouth, I felt a great sense of relief. The stress was finally over. I had feared failure greatly, but once it happened it wasn't so bad. Failure was not something I was used to. Or, at least, I thought. I had lived my life safely to avoid failure as a youth which resulted in me never trying. But, that was a failure in its own sense. Whether I had tried and failed, or never tried at all, I ended up in the same place.

Jason, the program director, would not accept my proposal.

"Dave, I'm hearing some mixed reviews of you from our field crews. But, what I'm hearing is that they believe in you. They believe you have potential and they are willing to work with you to find that potential. I know you have what it takes. I don't think working as an EMT for another year is going to get you where you want to be. There's only one thing you can do to improve and that's to get back on the medic unit and run more calls."

It was not the answer I was looking for. In the moment, I wanted the easy way out, but Jason was not going to allow that to happen. I left the meeting with a temporary boost in confidence. It was enough to get back on the medic unit that day and try to get through another shift, but deep inside I felt I was being sent down a longer path of failure. The inevitable future was only being postponed and I was not looking forward to the passage.

I sat on the medic unit for yet another shift wondering how I was still there. It was uncomfortable facing my fears and not accepting failure but Jason was right. There was only one thing I could do to make it better. I had to keep getting back on the medic unit. I had to keep running calls. The program director was not going to let me fail, and I did not want to fail my family. Even if I didn't see success in my future, others did. I didn't want to let anyone down. That's the only thing that kept me going.

Day of The Falls

I never bought into superstitions until I started working as a medic. Its belief was prominent in the medical field. A full moon brought out all of the crazies. Working with a partner who was a black cloud ensured you would remain busy running sick patients all shift. And, you didn't dare say the Q-word on a quiet shift or else all hell would break loose in the city.

Further in my career, I began noticing these strange coincidences. I felt we ran an increased number of psych calls at night when it was a full moon and there were certain partners that always seemed to get the sickest patients. But, after a new EMT decided to use the Q-word on shift, the city went to shit. A woman went crazy and rammed over twenty cars in a high-speed chase that ended in our district. Later that night, a guy flipped his car off an overpass while racing and died on impact. We had both of those responses after sitting quietly on a street corner for hours prior.

A trend I noticed early on in my career was that days would present with similar characteristics. Each day had a theme. In the span of my career, themes have ranged from patients who all had birthdays within weeks of each other to those who had all defecated themselves at some point during the call. There was morbidly obese day, drug overdose day, kids day, and on and on. But, it all started with the day of the falls.

Gravity was defeating the city. From kids tumbling on the school playground to the elderly slipping in the nursing home, we were getting all of the fall calls. Although the victims had been low acuity, I was still getting great experience asking the necessary questions to rule out a worst-case scenario.

Nearing the end of our ten hour day, we got a call for an older man who fell outside of a church. A large crowd gathered at the bottom of the concrete stairway just outside the front entrance.

The man was still awake and remembered missing a step resulting in his fall. There was a small pool of blood on the sidewalk which remained after loading the patient into our rig.

I carried on a normal conversation with the man and found out that he was the pastor for the church. He was very polite and courteous as we would expect given his title.

The pastor fell down six concrete steps, landing on his head on the way down. For what seemed like the tenth time that day, I asked the same question.

"Are you on any blood thinners?"

"I'm taking Coumadin for my heart," he tells me. The medication helps prevent blood clots which could build up as a result of an irregular heartbeat, but also has detrimental effects during an injury. I note the medication, but with the patient presenting stable, I had no reason to worry. I decide to take him in routine to the nearest hospital.

During the transport, I continue chatting with the man. The conversation soon goes from very formal to almost appearing as if he was intoxicated. His words become loosely chosen without regard. This wasn't right. He didn't sound like the same person we picked up initially. While talking, he begins to develop a slight slur in his speech.

"Say that again," I tell the patient, trying to confirm what I had just heard. My preceptor looks up from her report writing and stares at the patient in anticipation. She heard it too.

"Slaay Whuut Agaain?" the man slurs, laughing a bit.

"Are you hearing that?" my preceptor asks me.

I shake my head yes but am still frozen in my seat. A rush of thoughts enters my head as the man deteriorates right in front of me.

"What are you going to do? Are you making this a trauma or are we continuing on?" she asks, prying for me to make a decision.

I didn't answer her. I was still trying to think. I decided to check his grip strength first to better judge an overall picture of his neurologic status. If the man has a brain bleed as a result of his fall, it could be causing pressure in his brain which results in confusion, slurred speech, and weakness on one side of the body. He was weak squeezing both of my hands.

My preceptor looks at me. "Make a decision! Are we continuing or are you upgrading?" I was hoping for a clear-cut answer from my assessment, but decided to err on the side of caution anyways.

"Let's make this a trauma," I answer.

My partner shouts to the driver, "Step it up!" She rummages through a couple compartments and throws two IV bags and blood tubing at me.

"Spike the bags and call the hospital," she tells me.

I ask, "Can you spike a bag while I call?"

"No, you need to learn to do this on your own. Someday you will be the only one back here. You need to learn to be self-sufficient."

I was not used to calling for a priority return to the hospital. I sat on the bench seat with a phone pried up to my ear using my shoulder and both hands attempting to piece together IV bags. The phone rang briefly before a doctor answered the line.

"I have a code ten return to you guys for a fall with head injury," I begin.

"Go ahead," the doctor responds.

"Were coming in with a 74 year old male, he fell down six concrete steps and hit his head, he is on Coumadin, he is now altered and not making any sense, um, vitals are 176/74, heart rate 67, respiratory rate 20."

"What's your ETA?"

"Uh... three to five."

"See you in three to five." He hangs up.

I hang the bags overhead and grab an IV needle and tourniquet. The man has good veins for his age and the large needle inserts without an issue. I glance out the front of the rig, hoping to see the hospital in sight. We were downtown, but still had some ground to cover. The driver holds two fingers up through the opening of the cab signaling we have two minutes left. I throw the patient on high flow oxygen and prepare for my first trauma room report.

Denver Health is a large, teaching-hospital located in the heart of the city. When we brought in major calls, we were accompanied by physicians, resident doctors, imaging techs, respiratory therapists, nurses, EMTs, and anyone else who wanted to get an eye on the patient. Being the medic in charge of patient care put you on center stage. We were nearing the hospital and the driver signals one minute. The patient was talking but not making any sense. It's almost like he was in his own world. Amongst the circumstances, I can't help but second guess my decision to prioritize the transport. I feared entering the trauma room with my patient and being mocked by the more experienced staff for overreacting.

"Thirty seconds!" The driver broke my negative thinking. I glanced at my notes as we arrived. We wheel in to the trauma room. There is silence as we enter. Suddenly I am the spotlight in the largest hospital in Denver.

"Who's giving report? Let's go!" the trauma doctor demands.

"Alright, we have a 74 year old male, fell down six concrete steps landing on his head, negative loss of consciousness, he was alert and oriented on scene and began slurring his speech en route and is now disoriented to place and time, he is on Coumadin..."

As I start shouting report, the room begins swarming the patient and performing their duties. I try to continue over the orders being barked out by the trauma physician, but at this point everyone had stopped paying attention to me. A lady at the computer near the door made eye contact and took the remaining information.

I continued to stand at the door watching the scene unfold in front of me. It was magnificent watching such a professional and well organized team come in and take action as soon as the exchange was made. I get a pat on the back by one of the doctors as he leaves the room to contact surgery about a possible patient.

I walked back to the ambulance bay, feeling a partial sense of accomplishment and partial doubt. I still felt the fear of humiliation from my crew for bringing the patient emergent to the ER. He was sick and his status was changing, but he was not dead. I didn't want to look like I overreacted or got scared. Alone, I sat on the edge of the dock in front of the emergency department entrance and began writing my report.

The paramedic who drove came and joined me.

"Do you think I made the right decision to upgrade him?" I asked.

He tells me, "It could go either way, but I would have wanted to see a more drastic change in his mental status before making him a priority trauma. But, if you feel he was sick enough to warrant it, then you made the right decision."

The conversation didn't make me feel any better. For the next three days I kept wondering if I had made the right choice. Decision making on paper was easy. A wrong choice didn't affect a life, and there was no repercussion from your peers for getting a test question wrong. In the field, it was different. I felt that I needed to be one hundred percent on the streets in a program which allowed eighty percent on paper to be satisfactory.

A few days later, I received the assurance I was looking for. Follow up showed the patient was sent to neurosurgery for a brain bleed and was admitted to the Intensive Care Unit. I couldn't have been happier! I made a decision and it was the right choice. I was excited, but somewhere out there in the city was a family who was in despair.

The world had a weird way of creating balance. For every bad thing that happened, there seems to be an equal amount of good that came from it. The pastor's misery caused me to be more secure in my abilities as a medic and more confident in my decisions. And the previous patients who had fallen victim to the day of falls allowed me to be at the top of my game when the most critical of them was presented.

An Angel's Halo

I was thankful Jason wouldn't let me quit. Transitioning from EMT to Paramedic was a difficult hurdle to overcome, but the more experience I gained on the medic unit, the more comfortable I became. I started showing up wishing for critical calls. If I was going to make it on my own, I needed the experience of managing those scenes backing me. At the top of a stairway, alone in his home, one patient made my wish true.

   Returning home from grocery shopping, the man's wife found her husband collapsed. He was grey and was not moving. She called 911 and dispatchers advised her to start compressions. We showed up minutes later.

   We raced up the stairs with armfuls of equipment. My preceptor took over compressions and the driver worked on obtaining IV access. I was left with airway management and running the defibrillator. The positioning was an intentional move on my preceptor's part. The one at the head was in charge. That was me. I cut open the man's shirt and attach the pads to his chest.

"Direct us," my preceptor says. "What do you need?"

"Hold on, I got to see what rhythm he's in," I tell her.

I plug the pads into the monitor and direct my team, "Stop CPR."

Any movement being caused to the patient stopped and I got a clear look at the heart rhythm. It was ventricular fibrillation, a rhythm which we could shock.

"He's in V-fib," I shout out. I charge the monitor and prepare to defibrillate. "Everyone clear." I look to ensure no one was touching the patient. Scanning the body, I notice one of the firefighter's boots is touching our victim. "Move back," I tell him. He scoots back and I push the shock button.

The man's body jerks. Immediately the crew gets back on chest compressions.

"Let's push one milligram of Epinephrine," I order. The medic pushes the medicine that will help improve the heart's contractions and raise blood pressure throughout the body.

After two minutes of compressions, I have the team pause for another rhythm check. It hadn't changed.

I charge to two hundred joules and shock the patient again. "Continue compressions and give three hundred milligrams of Amiodarone," I direct my preceptors. "I'm going to tube him."

I reach into my kit and pull out the intubation bag and prepare to secure a breathing tube. As I gather equipment, I had a flashback from one of my first cardiac arrest calls. I was the EMT breathing for the woman with a bag valve mask. When the medics arrived, they pushed me out of the way and quickly secured a tube. I was excited. That was going to be me today.

I knew exactly what I needed to do. We had trained extensively on airway management and practiced securing tubes in the operating room on real patients, but today was going to be my first experience in the field. I bent over on one knee with a laryngoscope blade in my left hand and the endotracheal tube in my right. I inserted the blade into the patient's mouth, advancing it a bit until I reached the back of the throat. All I could see was soft tissue. I couldn't identify any landmarks. I pushed a bit deeper with the blade but still obtained no new results.

Oh, come on, I got to see something!

I pulled the blade back out a bit and reinserted, searching for the vocal cords. Still, there was the same view of soft tissue.

I gotta get this! I'm not letting this go. I have to get this tube!

The vision of the medic inserting the tube flashed before me again. This time I noticed something different. He wasn't bent over awkwardly on one knee tubing the patient like I was. He was flat on the ground on his stomach.

I quickly went prone, flattening my body to the hallway carpet and getting face to face with the dead body. I advanced the blade and like the glow of an angel's halo, the vocal cords come into view. I could almost hear the musical *Ahhhhh* play out as the light from my blade illuminated its landmark.

"I see cords!" I shout.

I hold the laryngoscope blade steady with my left hand, careful not to budge so I don't lose the picture I obtained. With my right hand, I steadily insert the breathing tube through the vocal cords.

As I pull the rigid stylet out, the driver secures the tube and my preceptor confirms its placement.

"Good breath sounds left and right, nothing epigastric, there's mist in the tube and colorimetric changes on end tidal," she confirms out loud. I know it's a good tube.

I had finally done it. For the first time I felt like a real paramedic. That is what I got into the field for. I wanted to make a difference in people's lives. I wanted to be there when they needed help and confidently manage their emergency. I wanted to have the skill to actually make a difference. I was floating in my own sensation of accomplishment, but we still had a job to do.

"We've got pulses!" I hear on our next rhythm check. The monitor shows a slow, but improved rhythm. Now we had two hundred and fifty pounds of dead weight to bring down the stairs and load into the medic unit.

THE MOST STABLE RHYTHM

Life was getting easier as I progressed through the program. The medics showed their serious side as I was proving myself, but eventually began to lighten up. They were no different than I had been on shift. They liked to joke around and give their partner shit. They goofed off and made fun of situations we had experienced throughout the day. It became comforting seeing a more human side to my trainers and finding a connection in our similarities.

We started watching movies on shift during any stretch between calls. I was finally able to relieve a bit of stress by taking the job off my mind and relaxing. It was nice knowing that I was being trusted and viewed as a competent student. Even if they didn't directly say it, they were showing it through their actions. I was being accepted.

Our movie was interrupted by a call for a man who appeared to be under the influence of drugs and was incredibly agitated. The call came from police who were attempting to subdue the subject.

We roll up on the scene surrounded with police vehicles and a crowd of spectators. Five officers had the man pinned to the ground. Even with the enormous force surrounding him, the guy was still fighting.

As we approach, we find a scrawny kid in his twenties at the bottom of the pile. He was jerking his body trying to free himself. Amongst the spitting and cussing, police were struggling to control him. It was almost as if he had super-human strength. The scene was intense.

The classroom taught us to wait for police to secure the scene before entering, but there was no time to sit back and wait. We were called to assist and it was up to us to use the tools at our disposal to bring the situation to a resolve.

"Let's give Haldol and Benadryl," I suggest. "Once he calms down, we can restrain him to the gurney." The game plan was set. The sedative effects of the anti-psychotic drug Haloperidol combined with the drowsy effects of Benadryl should have this patient in a state where he is no longer a threat. My preceptor headed back to the rig to get the medication.

I knelt down next to the fighting patient. There was no use talking to him. The sounds coming out of his mouth were more grunts and screams than actual words. He almost sounded possessed. I reached in and checked a pulse at his wrist.

"Be careful," one of the officers warn me. "He already bit one of our guys." I take caution and note he has a pulse present.

My preceptor returned. "How much are you going to give?" she asked, confirming that I knew the dose.

"Ten milligrams," I respond with the maximum dose allowed per our protocol, "and fifty of Benadryl."

She draws the medication into a syringe and hands the concoction to me. I work my way through the layer of struggling officers, needle in hand, ready to administer the sedative.

"Alright, I have the chemical sedation, I need his upper arm," I let them know. The officers work together forcing his arm outward. I find the muscle tissue and with a swift stab I inject the mixture into the jerking extremity.

The needle landed perfectly into the deltoid. I quickly pushed the syringe forcing the medication into the tissue. After retracting the needle from his arm, I slowly hand it off behind me for my partner to secure.

"It's in," I give everyone a heads up. "He should be good in five to ten minutes or so." My time in the danger zone was over. I took a step back to keep a healthy distance and let the officers do their job.

The medics work on placing restraints on the patient and I keep an eye on the effects of the medication. *Hopefully the sedative starts kicking in soon*, I wish.

I check his pulse rate again. It is still strong and very rapid. He's definitely worked up. It could be from fighting the officers or it could be from drugs. We didn't know for sure. All we did know was that his heart was ticking away as if he had just run a marathon.

Less than a minute had passed by when the officer closest to me made a comment that sent chills down my spine. He laughs a bit and said, "Wow! That stuff you gave him really works! He's barely fighting us at all."

Nothing good could have come from the timing of that comment.

I look. He's not moving. His body looks limp.

"Roll him!" I shout.

The officers grab the man and roll him onto his back. His flaccid body flops over revealing a blue tint to the lips of a face that was once vibrant and pink. His eyes were open and rolled back. His rapid breathing and grunting in rage turned to ineffective gasps for air.

"Oh, damn!" one of the officers reacts.

I check a pulse and it is still present.

"Get him up, get him on the gurney!" I order. The officers and firefighters work together to lift the lifeless body onto our stretcher. I make my way around the side door to get in position at the head.

My preceptor asks me, "What are you going to do now?"

As I rush to get in position before the patient gets loaded, I tell her, "I'm doing a nasal tube if he has a gag reflex, otherwise I'll just tube him."

"Okay," she says satisfied with my response.

The patient gets loaded in. I have my airway kit prepared and am ready to place the breathing tube. As the gurney gets locked in, I reach for the neck to check for a pulse one last time.

Nothing.

I feel again, in a different spot of the neck, but there is still nothing.

The man's body is lifeless. There is no breathing and the blue has spread throughout his face.

"There's no pulse!" I shout out.

"No pulse?" my preceptor confirms.

"No pulses. Start CPR."

Everything becomes a blur, as I call out orders to my team and race through my mind to find the next appropriate task. We hook the patient up to the pads and a flat line rolls across the monitor screen. He is in asystole. After pushing drugs, I insert a breathing tube and we roll out priority to the closest hospital.

I grab the phone to give our doctors a heads up that we were headed in with a critical patient. I look out the front window to see how close we are to the hospital, but only see a police vehicle with blue lights flashing escorting us through traffic. I look out the back and see three more cop cars following closely behind our ambulance.

Our police escort ends at the emergency department where the patient is pronounced dead.

I began wondering, C*ould it have been the medication that caused his death? It happened so quick after the Haldol was given*. My preceptor had the same concern.

After filling out police reports on the incident, we research the drug that was given. Haloperidol is like any medication in the fact that it has side effects. One of those side effects is that it prolongs a portion of the electrical conduction in the heart which could increase the possibility of the patient going into a deadly dysrhythmia. This could explain why the patient died right in front of us.

I keep telling myself that he probably worked himself up too much. With a mixture of psychotic rage and drugs that jacked his body up, his heart couldn't handle it. But, was that true or just a fabrication I was trying to feed myself in an attempt to feel better? Either way, it made me concerned about what I had documented on that police report.

I was worried that I would be called into court to testify on the case. I was nervous that my actions would be scrutinized. Through all of my worries, I knew there was nothing I could do to change it. It was an uncomfortable feeling, but feeling anxious about it didn't change a thing.

We returned to the ambulance garage out of service. The supervisor met us to further document our case as an unusual incident.

"Fill this out and then you guys are free to go home. I'm pulling your car. I think you guys went through enough for one day."

As students, we were scrutinized for saying a patient's vitals were 'stable' because it really gave no information without context. A person whose blood pressure stayed in a normal range was considered stable. Across the street in the education building, we used to joke that asystole was the most stable rhythm, because you couldn't get any worse and you typically didn't get any better. It was a point our patient proved.

It was an odd feeling not knowing whether or not your actions caused the death of somebody. Even though there was no intention, the result could still be linked through actions. I refused to take responsibility for his outcome. Even if it was our medication which stopped his heart, I kept thinking, *He did this to himself. He was probably on drugs. He decided to fight the police. He put himself in that position, not us. And he ended up where he was because of his actions.*

My intention was to calm him down and keep everyone else safe. Regardless of his outcome, I completed my objective.

TRAINING DAY

My final ride was with a man I respected throughout the program. He had been there through all of my ups and downs. He kept me motivated to continue on past the struggles and fear, even when I had given up on myself. Jason, the program director and veteran paramedic was going to be my final preceptor. Accompanying him was a supervising medic and educator who would be driving for the day. The selection for evaluation couldn't have been any more intimidating.

This was my training day. I had today and today only to show them what I was made of. I had watched as a quarter of my class had failed out of the program throughout the last eleven months. I did not want to get this far only to be denied graduation and certification. I knew I had made it here for a reason and was determined to prove I had what it took to be a Paramedic.

As it turned out, the shift was flawless. My experience to that point had allowed me to demonstrate my abilities. I showed effective communication while attempting to convince a patient with chest pain to be seen at the hospital after she was adamantly refusing. I showed off my clinical judgment when I determined a patient who had been involved in a car accident had a low blood sugar after he provided subtle clues to his disease. I handled the rest of my patient contacts for the day with confidence and organization. I had developed to the point my trainers were aiming for.

At the end of the shift, in the medic garage, Jason told me that I demonstrated proficient knowledge and had proven myself worthy of being signed off as a graduate of the program. He shook my hand and congratulated me on a job well done.

"See, I told you that you could do it!" he encouraged me. I was still somewhat in shock, but knew my hard work had finally paid off. It's difficult for others to believe in you if you don't believe in yourself. Somehow Jason always stood by me and pushed me to succeed even when I didn't see that the finish line was right in front of me.

Inside I was excited, but still nervous about what was ahead. The sick feeling in my stomach had never let up since the program started. I had not become comfortable, but that was expected. We were told by an experienced medic in class that it would take nearly four years before we actually became comfortable. Although, he also told us most medics become burned out within four years.

Jason and I walked across the street toward the education center which was next to the hospital. As we were nearing the emergency department, the sounds of sirens became more and more prominent.

"That's probably the guy who got hit by a vehicle from earlier," Jason says. "You want to go watch?"

"Yeah. Sure!"

We enter the emergency room just as the medic unit arrives. The crew rapidly wheel in a man who was mangled by a bus. He is bloody and bruised all over his chest and face. The medics move him over, unconscious and intubated.

The trauma doctor immediately asks for a chest kit.

"You'll want to see this," the nurse tells me as he leaves the room to gather equipment. He returns with a large sterile package wrapped in a blue covering. The kit is quickly opened and contents removed. The doctor and surgeon in the room prep the man's chest and begin sawing it open down the middle of his sternum. A clamp is inserted and the man's rib cage is pried apart exposing his heart and lungs.

Holy shit! I sit back observing with my eyes wide open now.

Blood begins pouring out of the chest cavity. The doctor reaches in and stimulates the heart manually. Their last ditch effort was ineffective. The man dies on the table and the attention in the room slowly dissipates. Soon, the only thing left is a white sheet covering the body.

I sit back still taking in the scene from the corner of the room. The nurse who brought the kit comes back to talk to me.

"Let me see your hand," he says.

I reluctantly open my hand as he reaches to place something in my grip. It is a small one-ounce measuring cup.

"You witnessed your first emergent thoracotomy."

"Well thanks. What is the glass for?" I ask, still confused.

"It's used for measuring something in the kit but no one ever uses it during the procedure. There's not enough time. I pulled it out before giving it to the docs. It's a shot glass. I got one the first time I saw someone get their chest cracked so I figured I would give one to you."

"I appreciate it, man. Thanks!"

"Have a shot for this guy, alright?" he tells me.

I was excited. Today was a day for celebration. I went home and started filling the chest kit glass with vodka. The first shot was in celebration for me passing my paramedic program. But more importantly, the next was in remembrance to the man who died allowing me to have this shot.

PARAMEDIC

Campfire Ghost Stories

The question I dreaded the most when I was new to the field was "What is the worst thing you have ever seen?" I hated being asked this question because it brought up emotional events in my mind that I didn't care to recall. Over the years of seeing the things I had seen, I became desensitized.

My wife and I were invited over by our neighbors to have a fire in their backyard and share some beers. We put the kids to bed, sank down in camping chairs, and relaxed for the evening with company.

My neighbor's wife was a registered nurse and worked at a facility in town. Even though she did not work in an emergency department, she still had an understanding of the medical field and what one had to go through to work in that field.

My neighbor was used to the stories his wife would bring home. His level of comfort built through the repeated exposure. That, and the combination of beer, had him feeling comfortable enough to ask me, "Have you ever seen a dead body before."

I laughed a little after he asked it. I wasn't sure exactly what he was looking for in the answer. Probably just a simple yes, but I decided to take it a step further and give him what he had asked for.

"Which time?" I respond.

I was feeling good after a couple of beers and open to the conversation. "I've seen a few," I tell him as I proceeded to describe in detail all of the memories of dead bodies which had housed themselves in my mind over the years.

"I had an old lady who died in her living room. I got to shock her but she didn't make it. Then we had a large lady who died while eating dinner and the medic pulled a large piece of bacon out of her throat. I had the woman who got crushed on the freeway and her car splint in half. She was just staring off into space but looked peaceful. That was actually my first dead body. We had the woman who died in her sleep and her young daughter found her in bed. When we rolled her she was stiff and cold."

My audience was quiet. They were either intrigued or shocked. I continued on.

"Let's see, there was the man we found dead in the morning in his trailer just laying on the floor. He was an old guy. Probably was his time. There was the man who collapsed in his kitchen and wasn't found until the next day. He was still propped up against the kitchen cabinet but his blood was all pooled towards the lower half of his body. There was the old woman in the nursing home that died in her sleep. There was this guy who was being restrained by the cops and died after I gave him some medicine to try and calm him down. Then, there was the guy who killed himself in a bathtub by hanging himself. He still had his hands clenched on the edge of the tub when we arrived..."

Sheila stopped me. "Dave, I don't think they want to hear about every dead body you've seen."

"What?" I say with a slight laugh. "I didn't even get to the cardiac arrest we had at the top of the stairs, that was my first intubation, or the woman who..."

She cuts me off again. "Dave, stop."

I get the point.

"Well, they wanted to know."

"No, no..." my neighbor says, "We did ask." They change the subject.

Or the kid that had the baby wipe shoved down his throat, I think. *Nah, they definitely don't want to hear that one.*

For the remainder of the night we had a good conversation.

Almost a Bad Day

The day had finally come. Internship was finally over and it was time to move on with the next step in my career. Today was graduation. I waited patiently with my classmates for my name to be called.

"David Stone."

Jason had the microphone. He set it down and began applauding as I made my way up the steps. I walked across the stage and shook each instructor's hand. The last was Jason who handed me my certificate.

"Good job, man!" he says to me personally with a smile on his face. He gave me a pat on the shoulder as I began to clear the stage. I looked back to the crowd where my family was seated and waved. It was official. I was a Paramedic.

Sheila and I got married during the program. Soon after I graduated, we moved back to our home state of Washington with our newborn son. I continued working for the same ambulance service, but this time in a new city with a new title. My old uniforms were handed in and I was issued crisp new ones with 'D. Stone, EMT-P' embroidered.

The new title brought new responsibly and new worries. It was anticipated. Even though I felt nervous stepping out on my own for the first time, I had plenty of experience backing me and knew I would survive as long as I remained dedicated. I put on a face of confidence and never admitted any lack of knowledge. I didn't dare show any weakness. I had seen how the streets could be. Any patient, firefighter, nurse, or even your partner would eat you alive if they had any doubts in your abilities. I looked forward to the day that I could be completely comfortable in my position. Until then, I had to act like I knew what I was doing.

We respond on the outskirts of our district for a man having trouble breathing. The area was covered by a volunteer fire department which meant I would be the only medic on scene.

I had been a medic for almost a month and had run a few sick patients. The experience was helping to get rid of some of the jitters, but it wasn't happening quickly enough. I had studied so much, I was sick of it. It was time to step into the field with both feet and find out what I was really made of.

We got on scene and found the man sitting bolt upright in his chair on the front porch. He was obviously struggling to breathe and looked anxious.

"Sir, can you talk?" I ask.

"Its... hard," he says, speaking only one word at a time before he runs out of breath.

"When did this start?"

"Just... now," he barely gets out. The information the volunteers on scene could gather was also lacking due to the severity of his condition.

I ask the patient, "Have you ever have problems breathing like this? Do you have COPD?"

He struggles out a, "No," while shaking his head.

Damn! I thought, hoping that the problem would be easily solved. I wanted to treat him now and get the call over with. I didn't want to play the guessing game in front of the family while the man was still struggling.

We need to start moving, my mental alarm sounds.

"Let's get the gurney right next to him," I instruct the volunteers.

I turn back to the patient.

"Do you have problems with your heart?"

"No," he barely gets out.

"Do you have any pain or pressure anywhere?"

He shakes his head, no. It doesn't look like he can talk any further.

I pull out my stethoscope and begin to listen to lung sounds. They sound clear.

I reach in to check a radial pulse and don't feel anything. I ask the volunteers, "What were his vitals?"

"70/40, but we were having a difficult time obtaining the pressure." With his dangerously low blood pressure, I know we have already spent too much time on scene.

"Alright, we need to move."

We load the patient onto the gurney and I attach the EKG monitor to his chest to get a detailed look at his heart. The rhythm is fast and wide.

Is that V-tach, I question myself. The strip showed a conduction pattern indicating the man's heart was distressed and beating ineffectively. If the blood wasn't flowing adequately, his pressure would drop. Everything was starting to make sense.

I immediately apply the defibrillator pads while running the information through my head again to reassure that I was making the right decision. The story and information we gathered made sense. The only thing left to do was to shock him back into a normal rhythm.

I couldn't help but second guess my decision. I felt the pressure.

Something needs to happen quickly, I think. *The patient will only get worse if I sit back and do nothing. And, what kind of a medic would I be if I can't make a treatment decision. I'm going to do it. I'm just going to shock him.*

I prep the monitor, but take a look at the rhythm strip one last time. Something was sticking out at me. I couldn't tell what it was. I kept looking, scanning over each lead. Finally, it came to me. *He's not in V-tach. His heart rate is 140.*

Memories from cardiology class came crashing down on me. Life-threatening symptoms from the dysrhythmia ventricular tachycardia typically occurred at heart rates over 150. His rate was too slow to qualify. *It must be his heart compensating for some other issue.*

"Are you going to cardiovert him," my partner asks in anticipation for all of the preparation I had done.

"No, I'm just going to prep him," I say. "I don't think it's his heart but if he deteriorates, I probably will cardiovert. I'm just going to treat him for respiratory and give him a bolus of fluids and see how he does."

I still couldn't help but second guess my decision.

Throughout the transport, I contemplate my treatment plan. *What if I screwed up and they cardiovert him in the ER? But, if I do cardiovert him and he doesn't need it, then what? I stop his heart for nothing? What if he dies?* Every scenario I ran through my head felt like the wrong answer. I was damned if I did and damned if I didn't. I look over the EKG again and try to come up with any reasonable evidence to sway my decision, but I can't find any. *I guess we will see when we get to the ER,* I tell myself.

My stomach felt sick from the stress of the call. Being on the verge of a decision that could have such a huge impact was not exhilarating at all. I wanted to help. The last thing I wanted to do was cause harm. The interventions I controlled had the power to do both. I didn't need permission to perform them. It was my responsibility to use good clinical judgment in every decision I made. That was the power and responsibility of being a prudent medic.

After transferring care, I discuss the call with the ER physician. He agreed with me that the patient did not need to be shocked. I was thankful that something out there kept me vigilant and led me to the right choice.

All day, I kept thinking, *you lucky son of a bitch, I almost shocked you!*

You'll Never Be the Last One

Mistakes were bound to happen. It was almost like a rite of passage. Every milestone in my career came with a new set of worries. It seemed like the only way to push past those worries was to experience it. Failure was inevitable, but it was the way we learned.

The passages in our books, the limitations in our protocol, and the requirements set forth by the state all came from one thing: learning from what didn't work in the past. It wasn't called practicing medicine for nothing. Our studies were geared to help us avoid errors, but no matter how many times something was read in a book the true teacher in life was experience.

Being in a new system where I was the only advanced level care on scene was far different than I had realized. I was used to having paramedics from the fire department on scene to bounce ideas off of and assist with prepping advanced equipment. Now, it was up to me to not only assess the patient, but also prep my equipment, calculate drug doses, and choreograph the scene.

We were called out for a patient who was having a seizure. The dispatch information was limited, providing only a street corner where the patient would be found. I immediately began stereotyping the call. *It's going to be a homeless guy in his fifties withdrawing off alcohol*, I assumed.

I knew what to do if the patient happened to still be in a seizure when we arrived. It was a standard dose of an anticonvulsant drug. All I needed to do was get an IV and I was golden. More than likely, the seizure would break on its own and we would be deciding whether or not the patient really needed transport. *This is going to be another easy call,* my thoughts continued as we blazed through the streets with lights flashing and sirens blaring.

When we arrived on scene, I see a daycare van stopped in the middle of the road at the intersection. A firefighter holding the body of an elementary school-aged girl comes at a fast-paced walk towards our rig. She was still seizing.

This was not what I was expecting. Immediately, my nerves kicked in. Child dosages are all weight-based which require math during the most critical point of a call. My partner races to the back and opens the doors for the crew. The firefighter steps in and places the little girl on the gurney.

Shit! They're already in the back waiting on me. I know I need to move quickly. I wished I had more time to prepare.

Stepping out, I spot the caregiver and shout, "How much does she weigh?"

"I don't know, I'm sorry," she responds with a look of sorrow. I could tell she really wanted to do something but felt helpless.

"How old is she?" I ask.

"She's six."

I pull out a reference guide from my front pocket and flip through until I find pediatric weights. I trace the line from age six. *Forty pounds.*

Forty pounds is about twenty kilos, I quickly calculate. *The dose for Valium is 0.2 milligrams per kilogram IV.* I run the equation on my glove and determine the dose is 4 milligrams. *If I can't get an IV, I can push Versed up the nose.*

My plan is set. I step in the back, get handed a small IV needle, and start searching for a site. A long vein running down the girl's arm sticks out to me and I go for it. The chamber fills with blood. Success! The IV is in.

As my partner checks a blood sugar from the sample collected off the needle, I go digging through my narcotic box. I easily spot the Valium. It is the only drug that is not packaged in a small vial. Its long slender container is distinct. With Valium in hand, I go looking for the device I need to attach in order to dispense it, but it is nowhere to be found.

"Where's the carpujet?" I ask my partner.

He looks around, digging through bins but can't find one. I search through the IV tray and cabinets but still come up empty.

Oh my God! You've got to be kidding me. I can feel the pressure as I frantically search. Everyone's eyes are on me as I display a lack of competency. We are supposed to be prepared. Not having the proper equipment stocked is unacceptable.

I look down at my patient. The girl is still seizing. There is nothing else anyone can do for her that hasn't been done already. The attention is on me to make a move. I am beyond my time limit. It was time to change plans.

I reach for the versed vial and run the calculation through my head. *Versed is 0.1 milligrams per kilogram IV.* I look down at my glove for the weight I wrote down earlier as I prepare a needle and syringe to draw up the medication. *Okay, that's 20 kilograms which means I can give a 2 milligram dose.*

The patient was still seizing. My partner began suctioning the foam and secretions from her mouth. Looking at her only distracted me from what I was trying to accomplish.

I looked at the concentration on the vial. *10 milligrams per milliliter. I need 2 milligrams which means I will be drawing up 0.2 milliliters into the syringe.* I insert the needle, draw up the medication, and place the empty vial in my back pocket.

I attach the syringe to the port on the patient's IV line and push two milligrams. Finally, the stress from the call was about to be over. I sat back and waited for the medication to take effect. But, our crew only sat there watching the girl continue to convulse. She needed another dose.

I slowly push the second dose for a total of four milligrams. Still, nothing changes. *Alright, I'm going for it all.* Without hesitation, I go for the third and final push. Six milligrams are in. The firefighters and I sit back and wait for victory. But all hope is lost as the girl continues her seizure.

What the fuck? I don't get it. The medication should have worked! I try to gather my thoughts and come up with, now, a third alternative plan.

We can't just sit here. We need to get going!

As I close my narcotic box, I notice I have a Morphine vial missing.

I must have dropped it somewhere, I think. But as I look closer, I notice I am not missing any Versed. My heart sinks.

Oh, fuck! I reach into my back pocket and pull out the vial I had just drawn up.

Morphine.

I want to just shoot myself. *God damn it! No! I did not just give the wrong medication did I?*

I re-read the label and my fears are confirmed. I just gave a high dose of narcotic pain medication to a seizing child.

I didn't know what to do. Part of me wanted to hide the mistake, but I immediately dismissed that thought. This was a field of integrity.

If I were to hide from this problem, I might as well hang up my cert. I wouldn't deserve to be here. No matter how uncomfortable it might be, I needed to come clean with my crew.

I look them in the eyes and say, "I screwed up, guys."

The rig was quiet. The patient was still seizing.

"I gave Morphine, not Versed."

"Okay," the fire Lieutenant responds. "We'll deal with it then." Her demeanor is reassuring. She steps in the back of the rig and sits down next to me on the bench seat. "What do you need to do?"

I felt defeated, but the job wasn't over yet. There was no option to quit. I had to pull myself together and keep moving forward.

"She needs versed," I say, grabbing the correct vial. I confirm it with the crew and push 2 milligrams of the medication. Immediately, the little girl's seizure stops. I was extremely relieved for the patient which only opened up room for me to worry about myself.

My career is over, I think. *I wasn't made for this position.*

"We better call the doctor," the Lieutenant interrupts my thoughts. "Do you want me to call?"

"No, I'll do it," I tell her. As much as I wanted to avoid the uncomfortable situation, I had to take ownership. On the phone, I give the hospital a heads up to our situation.

The girl's breathing is slow and shallow due to the heavy load of narcotics now in her system. Each breath brings in an adequate amount of oxygen so we hold off on giving her the antidote for the opioids. I closely watch her breathing until we make it through the emergency room doors and transfer care.

A room of eager faces awaits us. I give my handoff report to the nurses and doctor.

"We have a six year old girl, status seizures with history. She was seizing on our arrival and for about five minutes prior. We established a line and I did have a med error. She has six milligrams of morphine and two milligrams of versed onboard. The seizure stopped after the versed. She is breathing twelve times a minute and shallow but we have not had to assist..."

I prepare for the backlash. All sorts of scenarios run through my head. *Will they chew my ass out on the spot? Will they take me to a private room? Will they push this up the chain and notify the state?*

What actually happen, I could not explain.

The head physician in the emergency department gave me a pat on the back. He tells me, "Hey, don't beat yourself up over this. She's doing just fine now. Her body is probably used to all of those narcotics constantly circulating through anyways so she could handle it better than anyone else here."

I look at him, feeling confused but soaking in the words and not about to speak.

"Don't worry about it. These things happen. Just try and be more aware of your actions in the future. You weren't the first person to do this, and you won't be the last."

Weeks past by and I still couldn't get the image of the little girl out of my mind. I felt horrible every time the thought came back. I remained silent about the whole ordeal and hoped that my partner kept his mouth shut too. I didn't need ridicule from my own people. It was best that anyone who wasn't involved didn't know about it.

Everyone makes mistakes. The difference lies in the ones who learn from those mistakes and strive to better themselves in the process. My biggest failure helped build toward my strength as a medic. It wasn't something I was going to learn in a textbook. I needed to develop my ability to think clearly under pressure, and that only came through experience. It was failure which caused the nerves to go away, because I had finally experienced what I had feared. Once it was over, the fear went away.

Over the next few weeks, the sick feeling in my stomach slowly dissipated. My partner and I continued running calls without issue. I was able to find my normal routine and was beginning to get comfortable once again. The system was busy as I was writing my last patient report in the hospital lounge and my partner prepared our gurney for the next call.

Before I could finish, we got called out to a 911 response for child at a middle school having seizures. We pull up to the front of the school and park the rig. My partner and I get out to grab the gurney, but as we open the doors we discover the back of the rig is empty. There is no gurney.

I immediately look at my partner. It was his responsibility to put the bed back after our last call.

"Where's the gurney?" I ask him.

"Umm, shit! Did I leave it at the hospital?" The look of terror crosses his face as he realizes the mistake he just made. "Shit! I left it at the hospital! What do we do?"

"We can call another ambulance in. Or, we might be able to transport on the bench seat." I suggest. "Let's just go in and see if the kid even needs to be transported."

My partner takes a deep breath. "Alright, I don't want to have to call another crew in, though." I didn't blame him. I knew exactly how he was feeling.

"Let's just go inside and see what we have," I say as we walk in empty handed.

The Lieutenant watches us as we enter the scene without a stretcher. He gives us report on the patient explaining that the kid was wheelchair bound and had history of seizures. The school nurse confirmed that the convulsions stopped on their own without medications.

The Lieutenant followed up by saying, "So, go ahead and grab your gurney and we will load him up."

I motion for the Lieutenant to step away from the school staff and quietly tell him, "We got a little problem."

That's all I had to say. He already knew. "You guys left your gurney at the hospital, didn't ya?"

I shake my head, yes.

He walks out to the ambulance with us to discuss a game plan, but also to give us some shit.

"Alright, which one of you screwed up," he says in a joking manner. I look at my partner but keep my mouth shut.

He fesses up.

The Lieutenant began laughing. "You know you're not the first one of your colleagues to do that," he says, as he goes into a story about a time he made the same mistake. "I was on a call on the medic unit where we get to the back of the ambulance and I forgot to put the gurney back," he says, smiling. "Yep, left it at the damn hospital. So we just put the patient on the bench seat. Let her lay down and everything. We transported her back to the same hospital where I left the bed originally. We dropped her off, got our gurney, and didn't say shit to no one."

We were happy the Lieutenant was light about the situation.

"I think this kid will sit just fine on the bench seat," I say.

"Alright, let's wheel him out here and we'll act like everything is completely normal," the Lieutenant says.

We go forward as planned. The only issue was that the kid needed to be transported to a children's hospital. There was no way we could take him where our gurney had been left.

The plan was working. We transport the patient without any difficulties, but were forced to advise our dispatch center that we needed to head to the other hospital to retrieve equipment after the call.

While we were running our call, the supervisor got word that an abandoned gurney was sitting at a hospital with no ambulances in the bay. Our dispatcher also notified the supervisor that our unit was diverting from our assigned location to retrieve equipment at the same location. The puzzle pieces came together.

I expected my partner would just get ridiculed for his error. Instead, our management launched an investigation to determine why the bench seat was used for transport and why another ambulance was not called to the scene to bring a gurney.

After being interrogated in the supervisor's office, we were placed back in service to cover our district once again.

I was pissed.

"You know, it's amazing that you get so much shit about leaving a gurney at the hospital, which by the way I have heard of people doing multiple times since I've been an EMT, and I get a pat on the back for overdosing a little fucking girl!" I say in frustration. "They act like this wasn't a simple fucking mistake! You're not the first one that's left a gurney at the hospital and you know you won't be the last one either..." I found myself saying.

IF SHE DIES, SHE DIES

It was only a matter of time before I got introduced to the dark side of EMS. There was a facade placed over the reality of what I was dealing with. I had been too emotionally involved in the patient's condition and had been gauging my abilities as a medic based off their outcome. If I was able to turn a sick patient around, I was satisfied but still felt the scene could have played out better. If the patient deteriorated, I took personal responsibility. It was a dangerous slope which would only lead to more depression and disappointment. And it didn't help knowing I had committed a blatant error on my last critical call.

I had a heart. I saw my patients as people. I envisioned them with families and those who loved them. In the moment of their crisis, these people were relying on me to make them better. I didn't want to let them down. I couldn't handle looking a patient in the eyes and watching them deteriorate. Even if I had done everything in my capacity at the time, my mind still told me I should have performed better.

I needed separation from my emotions. If I was to continue working successfully in this field, I needed to look at them as subjects, not people. I didn't want to feel heartless, but I also didn't want to be mentally destroyed either. I had to clear my mind from the emotional thoughts that destroyed my performance and caused mistakes.

I finally understood the attitude necessary to survive. It was summed up to me in five short words by a medic I assisted on my next critical call.

"Respond non-emergent for a man down..." dispatch told us on the radio, directing us to the intersection where the patient was reported sleeping on the sidewalk. This was a typical call. More often than not, it was a member of our homeless population who drank too much and passed out in public. We had run this call many times before.

One of the few engine companies in the city which staffed a paramedic was closest to respond. We were stopped at a red light about ten blocks away from the call hoping we would get cancelled by the first incoming crew. As we sat there, a police car came burning through the intersection with its lights flashing.

"I wonder if he's going to the same call we are." I innocently ask my partner.

"Well, unless he knows something we don't..." my partner states the obvious.

Just then, our radio lights up. "Send us a medic unit priority for a possible shooting." We immediately flip on the emergency lights and clear the intersection. My partner speeds to the scene, pushing past the police barricade, and stops in the middle of the road.

A crowd of people surround the body lying on the pavement. The engine company's paramedic kneels at the head of the girl who appears to be in her twenties. She is extremely pale and obviously not breathing. The medic bags the patient while directing the scene.

"What do you need?" I call out.

"Backboard," the medic shouts.

We throw the patient onto the board and quickly move her to the ambulance. There is no question as to who is in charge of this scene. The medic demonstrates such authority that everyone looks up to him for the next move. He orchestrates the call smoothly and keeps everyone informed of the next step. It was an example I could look up to.

He points to me and calmly says, "Get me an IV." I nod my head and get to work.

He tells his EMT, "Check a pulse. If there is no pulse then start CPR."

He's not intense. He almost sounds dull as he speaks, like he's mocking our training videos. His level of experience is obvious. My partner starts stepping in the side door to see how he can help. The medic looks at him and says, "You. Drive!"

As soon as the rig begins to move, the medic addresses the entire crew working on the patient.

"Alright, everybody just relax. She's doing fine so we can all chill. Driver, just give us an easy ride to the hospital." He directs his attention back to us. "We're cool. If she dies, she dies. That's not our fault."

The girl caught a bullet to the lower part of her chest, possibly through the lung. There wasn't too much blood on scene and the wound had been sealed with an occlusive dressing. We continue working the patient. The medic effortlessly places a breathing tube. Everything is going fast as we make progress toward the trauma center.

I try for a line and miss. The girl's arms are so scarred up from needle use it makes insertion difficult. Not to mention that the ambulance movement on the road, the EMT pumping on the girl's chest, and the limited space in our environment made everything else challenging. The medic at the head attempts to put an IV in the girl's neck, but his attempt is also unsuccessful. Within minutes, we were relieved by the emergency department's trauma team. The girl was pronounced dead.

After the call, the fire department's medic gathered us in for another word.

"Well, that call didn't go very smooth, and it never will. Good job guys."

This call, and the attitude demonstrated by the medic, put many things into perspective for me.

If she dies, she dies.

Even through our best efforts, the patient may not survive. It's nature. It wasn't a reflection on my skill as a medic. I didn't put the patient in the situation they were in. I wasn't responsible for their emergency. And, things didn't always go right in the back of the rig. That was life. There were many variables affecting our ability to perform.

Not every call had to go smoothly because they rarely did. But, we still did everything we could to make a difference.

Four Loco

"That call didn't go very smooth, and it never will." I thought about those words over and over. The phrase kept racing through my head. It made me reflect on previous patients where things hadn't gone perfect. I had beaten myself up over little problems which were out of my control. This led to greater anxiety on calls by being fearful of any difficulty I may encounter. It was a downhill slope which only led to more and more mistakes. My personality strived for perfection and control. When things weren't going as I had planned, I felt a loss of control. It was going to be an uphill battle to overcome, but I was starting to understand how to improve and become a great medic.

  The battle wouldn't be won soon enough. I understood the concept but its application was difficult.

  It was two in the morning when our unit got called out to an apartment for an unresponsive male. As we entered the complex, a family member frantically waived us in the right direction.

The man was lying on the floor passed out but still breathing. I gave him a sternal rub with my knuckles to inflict a painful response. He groans a bit, but doesn't fully awaken. There were beer bottles everywhere and a pile of vomit next to his body.

"What's the story?" I ask the Lieutenant on scene for a handoff report.

"Our guy here has been drinking... a lot," the Lieutenant starts.

"What's he been drinking?"

"Uh, four loco is what the family is telling us." The look on my face told that I had never heard of the beverage. "It's like a tall malt liquor can. There are some of them over on that table."

I look over and the table is lined with similar cans. Everyone in the home had been drinking, so there was no telling how many our patient had at a quick glance. My guess was one too many.

"Has he been responding to you?" I ask.

"Yeah, somewhat. He tried to get some words out earlier but he's pretty intoxicated. His vitals are good and so is his blood sugar."

"And he puked?" I confirm.

"No, actually they said that wasn't from him."

"That's not his puke?" I say in disbelief. I walk over to the patient and roll him off of his side. He has vomit smeared on the front of his shirt.

"Let's get him loaded."

We pick the patient up off the floor and place him on our stretcher. As we start rolling out the door, he begins gagging. He lunges his body over the side of the gurney and hits his head on the doorframe as he begins dry heaving loudly. I quickly step to the side of the gurney to prevent him from tipping over. As he settles down, we adjust the patient back onto the gurney and get him out to the rig.

No vomiting, huh? I think on the way out the door. I was just glad that he woke up enough to clear his own airway.

As we load the patient, a firefighter steps in and asks, "What do you want us to do for you?"

"Could you spike me a bag?" I ask. The firefighter prepares the IV fluids.

My partner grabs a set of vitals while I attempt an IV. As I begin sticking the guy's arm, his mouth fills up with vomit. This time, he doesn't move.

"Roll him! Roll him!" I shout. The open needle goes missing from the man's arm as we try and allow gravity to clear his obstructed airway.

"Suction!" I call out. My partner is on it. He grabs the tubing and attempts to open the patient's mouth, but it won't budge. His teeth are clinched shut.

My partner informs me, "It won't open!"

"Won't open?" I ask quickly. My partner shakes his head, no.

I reach in and try to pry the mouth open with two hands but it won't budge.

"Keep him on his side. I'm going to have to RSI him," I say.

Rapid sequence intubation involves both sedating a patient and paralyzing them to facilitate placement of a breathing tube. The patient's gurgling breathing indicated he still needed to be suctioned, but we didn't have access through the mouth for the suction catheter and I still didn't have an IV for the paralytic. I became flustered with the overload of tasks I needed to accomplish. Without the medication, it was going to be very difficult to manage his airway. And without an airway, the patient would die. I was way behind the eight ball.

My immediate thought was to get an IV. I started grabbing equipment until I thought about how long the process would actually take. The patient didn't have that much time. The alternative was to try a blind intubation.

I ditch the IV equipment and instead reach into my intubation kit. I pull out a smaller breathing tube and begin inserting it through the patient's nose. I can hear gurgling through the end of the tube as I advance. Timing the respirations, I push the tube through as soon as

I felt I was in the right spot. I begin bagging the patient through the tube but only get confirmation of air movement over the stomach. The attempt was unsuccessful. Repeated attempts yield the same results, so I pull the tube and start again from square one.

I return to the arm to get an IV. While inserting the needle, I get blood flow in the chamber indicating successful placement. I retract the needle leaving the catheter in place, but in the haste one of the firefighters accidently pulls the IV out.

I became frustrated. *That was a good stick. Now it's gone.* I felt out of control. Everything I had tried for this patient resulted in failure. I couldn't think straight. I didn't know what move to make next. My confidence in managing the patient was shot. I had defeated myself. I was in the middle of a huge fucking mess that I needed to get out of.

I remembered the words of my EMT instructor: *Take a deep breath and go over your ABC's.* I needed to refocus my attention on the basics and gain control over this call. It wasn't over. He wasn't dead yet. *Airway, breathing, circulation.*

We had spent too much time on scene. I instructed my partner to start driving us priority to the hospital.

If he dies, he dies, I think. *It's not my fault. I didn't cause this. He did.*

I take a deep breath and attempt and IV in the neck. The line goes in. I hold the catheter tight and ask the firefighter to hand me the tubing. This time, I secure the line myself.

I call the hospital as I draw up the paralytic.

"We're bringing you a thirties male, intoxicated and unresponsive, he's vomiting and can't protect his airway, I'm going to tube him, see you in five, bye," I blurt out, not even waiting for a response. I toss the phone and push the drugs.

As the patient's body becomes paralyzed, his breathing stops and jaw relaxes. I lightly spread the patient's teeth apart and suction his mouth completely. I insert the laryngoscope blade used to visualize the vocal cords, sweep the tongue out of the way and advance until I reach my landmark.

I try to get my body in a better position to view the cords but the back of the rig is cramped. I try to insert the tube but can't seem to find the right angle to push past the vocal cords. I try again, but the tube keeps getting caught in the wrong position. I push a bit harder, determined to get it in.

Through my struggle, I look up in despair as the lights from the hospital become visible. It was time to prepare for our exit. I pull the tube, grab a bag valve mask and start breathing for the patient.

After giving a report to the attending physician, he quickly secures a breathing tube. I wanted to go home. I didn't want to have to suffer through the rest of my shift in defeat. If I went home, though, I didn't think I would ever come back. I just prayed that we would have an uneventful night, because I knew my mind wouldn't be in the game.

The next morning, I told my wife the story of my disaster. She tells me that every call I get gives me the opportunity to make a difference in someone's life and reassures me that I probably did everything I could for that patient. I agree with her to a point but inside I knew it should have gone better. I didn't want to come home with stories of my failure.

With the thoughts constantly running through my head, there was only one way I could surely get rid of them. I drove to the convenience store to grab some beer. After looking through the aisles, I found the perfect beverage.

A tall can of Four Loco.

I got home, cracked open the can, and took my first sip in remembrance of the unconscious man who had been occupying my thoughts for the past few days. I immediately spit it out.

"Ugh! This shit is disgusting!"

I couldn't stomach it. I ended up dumping the can in the sink.

WHEN YOU START THINKING ABOUT YOUR KIDS

It was the middle of the night when normal people were sleeping. My partner and I were wide awake watching the movie Stepbrothers, not daring to fall asleep. There was no point. We were busy the entire twenty four hours and could only guarantee maybe forty five minutes of rest between calls in the middle of the night. It wasn't enough sleep to be useful. It only made you groggier and angry that you were being wakened. I felt more effective pulling all-nighters, so I insisted on staying up the entire shift and sleeping at home. I needed to be at the top of my game to avoid making any more mistakes.

   As the sun came up and the city came to life, a call went out for chest pain. We respond to a cardiology clinic and were escorted to the patient by staff.

   "He's in V-fib," we are told.

"V-fib?" I ask. "We were told chest pain." My partner and I look at each other in excitement. Knowing ventricular fibrillation of the heart only occurs in cardiac arrest, we knew we were about to run a code.

We pick the pace up. After being led to the exam room, we find an incredibly pale but conscious man sitting in a chair. He is already hooked up to the clinic's EKG monitor and obviously not displaying the deadly rhythm. Instead, the patient was in V-tach which is still not a great situation, but at least we had time to fix the problem before it got worse.

We switch gears once again from our line of thinking and start treating the patient accordingly. My partner grabs a blood pressure and I go for a line. The pressure comes back at 106/88 with a heart rate of 200. I attach the defibrillator pads, but decide to hold off on cardioverting him while his blood pressure is adequate. My first plan was to give him an antiarrhythmic medication to convert his heart rhythm chemically. If that didn't work, I was going to have to shock him.

"How do you feel?" I ask the patient.

"My chest is tight and I feel dizzy," he says.

I give the man some aspirin tablets to chew up and load him on our stretcher. We head off priority to the nearest ER and I finally get to introducing myself.

"Hey, sorry everything happened back there so fast and I didn't get a chance to explain anything to you. So, you are in a bad heart rhythm and that is why you are not feeling good. I have a medication called Lidocaine that will hopefully get you out of the rhythm and make you feel better."

He cuts me off, "And what if that medication doesn't work?"

"Well, we have a few other options we could try. If I need to, I can shock your heart with the pads, but trust me, I will put you to sleep first so you don't have to remember that."

I take another blood pressure and it is 98/68. His pressure is dropping.

"I'm going to give you medicine that will hopefully get you out of this rhythm, okay?"

He says, "Okay."

I push the antiarrhythmic drug through his veins and closely watch the monitor for any change, but the rhythm continues. The patient anxiously watches alongside.

"How does your chest feel?" I ask.

"The same," he says. He looks up at me. "It didn't work?"

"I gave you the minimum dose and no, it didn't work. I'm going to increase the dose and see if it has any effect. If not, we're going to move on to something else."

The man begins to tear up. As I pull another pink box out of the med kit, he asks me, "Do you have any kids?"

I say, "Yes."

"How old are they?"

"One's three and the other is six months," I tell him.

Through his tears, he begins talking about his children.

"I have three kids. Well, they're all a lot older than yours. They have all moved away from home and I just don't get to see them as much as I would like."

In his head this man was facing death, especially after the first failed attempt to convert his heart. He began realizing the reality of the situation.

"I really wish I would have seen them more lately. My oldest has a granddaughter, you know?"

"I hear you, man. Let's give you this dose and get your heart back to a normal rhythm, alright?"

I assemble the second syringe and quickly push the medication.

Right after the drug is pushed, he says, "Whoa, what did you give me?" He starts to grab his head. "I'm starting to feel really dizzy."

"Really?" His response catches me off guard. I immediately look at the monitor. My fear was that his heart rate worsened or stopped completely. The image on the monitor was a beautiful normal sinus rhythm at 88 beats per minute.

"Hey look, your heart rate slowed down!" I tell him. "How does your chest feel now?"

"My chest feels fine now. I can feel it a little but its better," he says, looking extremely relieved.

A team of doctors and nurses wait in the ambulance bay for our arrival. I give my report to the room as the patient is transferred to his bed. The doctor in charge of the room jokes around with me after care is transferred. "Man, you got to do all the fun stuff."

I just smile and soak it in.

The look of comfort and relief on the man's face after his rhythm converted was something I had never experienced. The reality of death had encompassed him. He thought about his love and joy in life and immediately had regrets. It made me think about the people I loved and cared about in life. It also made me think about what I was missing out on as a result of my line of work. I was ecstatic about my trade, especially in moments like this, but I had to sacrifice my own family in the meantime.

That morning, I got to come home and share a story of victory. My wife tells me that she has never seen me look so passionate about something before. It made me realize how much I really did love being a medic. This was the first time I truly believed I made a difference. In this field, those moments were rare, but the reward was substantial.

THE GOLDEN HOUR

My goal as a paramedic was to have a zero minute on scene time. Time management was critical in our line of work and the only period I had control over was the amount I spent between response and transport. On a medical call, I preferred to move toward the ambulance because it is where I felt most comfortable. It was my environment where I had all the equipment I needed readily available, and if the patient crashed we were ready to transport rather than having to move a body. It kept us ahead of the curve when it came to the progression of a call.

In a trauma victim, the golden hour was adapted as standard. Victims with life-threatening injuries had increased odds of survival if they made it to a trauma center within one hour of their incident. We were trained to spend no longer than ten minutes on scene because victims of trauma needed a surgeon more than they needed a medic.

We got dispatched out as a second-in transport unit for a rollover accident in a neighborhood. We weren't expecting to see much given that we were the last unit called to the scene. That usually meant we would only get the leftovers. The narrow streets and random roundabouts did not allow much speed to be obtained, so we figured any injuries would be minor at best. But, this also wouldn't be the first time the citizens of this great city exceeded our expectations.

Two young girls were driving home drunk after leaving the club. While speeding through the neighborhood streets, they ran into what I coined as a 'drunk catcher.' These roundabouts were placed in poorly lit intersections on low-traffic routes for reasons I am unsure of. Stopping drunk drivers seemed to be their only useful purpose. The roundabout caused their car to roll over, tossing the two unrestrained occupants within the vehicle.

With our emergency signals lighting up the neighborhood, we notify the on-scene engine company of our approach. To our amazement, there was no other ambulance on scene. Somehow, we beat the first incoming unit.

"Park in front of engine two. We have a trauma patient with altered mental status," the Lieutenant informs us.

"Hell yeah!" I say to my partner. "We're getting the altered patient!" We drive by the rolled over vehicle and park in the designated location. "Alright, let's get in and out, real quick," I tell him.

We grab our gurney and wheel it up to the patient. The fire crew had already extricated the victims and secured them to backboards. We walk up, lift the patient onto our gurney, and place her in the ambulance. She had a noticeable wound to the head, but was awake and talking.

"You need a rider?" one of the Firefighters ask.

"Yeah," I tell him. "Give me a rider and we can take both patients."

"Are you sure? We have another unit responding that can take the second one."

"We'll be fine," I assure them. We scoot the first boarded patient from the gurney to the bench and the fire crew loads our second victim.

"You need anything or are you ready to go?" my partner asks, as I hop in the back.

"I'm good. Let's go priority."

The girls lay on their backboards quietly. They try to respond to my questions but can't come up with logical answers. Mentally, they are completely out of it. I grab each an oxygen mask and tell them, "Hold this up to your face and breathe into it." I didn't have much time to secure it correctly and needed my hands free to assess each victim. I also wanted a visual cue incase either went unresponsive. If the mask fell, it was obvious they were out.

The firefighter began spiking IV bags as I call the hospital and prepare my equipment.

"We're priority with two trauma activation patients, both were unrestrained and rolled their car, both are altered at this point. We have them c-collared, backboarded, working on an IV, I'll see you in five, any questions?" I quickly spit out.

"No, we'll see you in five."

Both girls looked equally severe so I chose to work on the most difficult angle first. I pump up the blood pressure cuff on the girl lying on the bench seat and quickly palpate a pressure. The heart rate felt normal but her breathing was rapid. I pump up the cuff a second time to double it as a tourniquet and insert the large bore IV needle. It goes in easy. Moving to the second, I quickly check a pulse to confirm an adequate pressure and move straight to the IV. I secure the line right as we enter the ambulance bay. As we wheel the patient towards the awaiting trauma team, I gather my thoughts in order to give a fluent report.

The emergency room doors open and the charge nurses tell us, "Well, that was a quick five minutes!" The room I anticipated to be full of doctors, nurses and other specialists was empty. The trauma team was still assembling.

"Yeah, that wasn't anywhere close to a five minute transport," my partner sides with the nurse.

"Apparently we were closer than I thought," I respond. It felt quick, but I had no idea how much time had actually passed.

"The medics are here? Where are the doctors?" another nurse asks.

"Probably five minutes out," I respond with a smile.

"Not funny," the charge nurse says. She looks serious.

I thought it was funny.

Sometimes when I have a lot on my plate, I go into autopilot with other tasks that I'm not currently focusing on. A five minute ETA to the hospital was my standard answer. If I would have thought before I spoke, I would have remembered that the call occurred only blocks away from the trauma center. I knew that going into the call but somewhere in the middle, autopilot took over.

My wife always said I can't multitask. She was right. There were days she would jokingly question how I even functioned as a paramedic. I told her I got paid to pretend like I knew what I was doing. I could laugh about my weakness because I was confident in my strengths. I would tell her, "I go on autopilot, but the problem is that it just runs the airplane into the ground."

Eventually the trauma team arrived. I gave report and head off to the EMS lounge.

"Man, that charge nurse was pissed at my comment. Where are the docs? Probably five minutes out," I laugh to my partner, mocking the situation.

"Yeah, really. Get a sense of humor, seriously," he responds, shaking his head. We walk into the lounge.

I check my pager to document times for my patient care report.

On Scene: 02:34. Transporting: 02:35. Arrived: 02:38.

"Damn!" I say to my partner. "We had a four minute on scene to trauma center time!"

Monday Morning Quarterback

On emergency scenes, no matter the outcome, there was always someone challenging the decisions you made. Certain medics felt necessary to prove themselves more dominant than the rest by saying they would have made a better decision in the same circumstances. These are the Monday morning quarterbacks.

They never admit to doing any wrong in their career. They are all knowing once the facts have presented themselves. Their ego is fed through hypothetical situations. All I can say is actually experiencing the dynamics of a call is far different than critiquing it after the fact. People think differently when they are under pressure. Fast decisions have to be made when seconds count. And, only the people who were actually there can vouch for the decisions that had to be made.

We respond to a head-on collision on a busy highway leading out of our district. The area was covered by a volunteer department who was used to running major incidents on this stretch of roadway.

Businesses lined the shoulder resulting in vehicles frequently crossing traffic. With an understanding of the location and the dispatch information, we had a good idea what we were getting ourselves into.

The scene looks hectic. The two vehicles involved had hit head on and both suffered massive damage. A small pickup rested on the shoulder with its front and driver side caved in. The SUV took the blunt of the damage head-on and was sitting in the middle on oncoming lanes. As we pull up, firefighters were working on extricating victims from the mangled SUV.

I look around the scene to see who is in command. As I scan the wreckage, I notice a tarp over a body in the front seat of the SUV. Rescuers were using cutting tools to gain access. I look across the highway and see personnel shuttling back to retrieve medical equipment from bags placed on the ground. I look further over toward the shoulder and see a firefighter talking with two more possible victims.

My concentration was broken when a man's voice shouted out, "Hey, are you a medic?"

"Yeah, I'm a Paramedic," I identify myself to the man in a red helmet, indicating a position of rank.

"Good," he says in relief. "We have two victims in that SUV and we're working on getting the front seat passenger out now. The other two are standing on the shoulder."

"How are they doing inside the car?" I ask.

"They were unconscious," he responds.

"Are they breathing?" I ask.

"Yes, they're breathing. They were in and out consciousness though."

"Okay," I respond.

"Four victims total?" I confirm.

"Yes, four victims. What resources do you need?" the commanding officer asks.

I look over to the shoulder once again to get a visual of the remaining two victims. The male was holding pressure on his face but was still standing. The female appeared to be answering the firefighter's questions and was also standing on her own beside the male. Being in a situation with multiple victims and limited resources changed things, but I still knew exactly how I wanted to proceed.

"I can take one red," I say, identifying one of the unconscious victims from the SUV. "Whoever you guys get out first, I don't care. I want one ambulance for the other red and one for the two walking wounded over there. They can double load the greens," I tell him.

"You got it."

Command calls in a request for two more units as I walk over to check on the upright couple.

"Hey, what's your name?" I ask the male, identifying myself as a paramedic. He responds appropriately and so does the girl after being asked the same question. They seemed to be processing information appropriately, which was great given the extent of damage their small truck took.

"Are you guys both from the pickup?" I question her.

"Yes." I begin cross referencing their answers to get a better picture of their mental state. The couple passes my test no problem. I check a quick pulse on both. They are strong and regular.

"Where are you guys hurting?"

The girl answers first, "I'm hurting in my neck and back and my knee is really sore."

The guy follows up, "My face hurts but other than that I think I'm okay."

"Yeah, you look like you took an impact to your face," I tell him, looking at his injuries. "So, we still have two trapped in the other vehicle. I need to go check on them. Will you guys be okay here for a bit? We have more medics on the way to check you guys out further and get you to the hospital."

"We'll be fine," they tell me.

As I return, the engine crew had peeled the roof off of the SUV. We place a backboard to help extricate the victim from the passenger seat. With the roof of the vehicle removed, we were given easy access to slide her rearward and up to escape the damage surrounding her. Without strapping her down, we move through the scene to the back of the ambulance.

The young girl from the SUV that I transported did not suffer life-threatening injuries. Neither did her passenger. They were knocked unconscious from the heavy impact, but were awake during extrication. Besides gashes to the face and bruising to the body, neither suffered any major injury.

Many of my co-workers had been discussing the call around headquarters. It was amazing how people who were never involved knew so many of the details. Days after the incident, an experienced medic on our crew called me out on my transport decisions. This medic had transported the couple standing on the side of the road and later found out that the guy had to be transferred to a hospital in Seattle for fractures around the eye.

"Yeah, that boy should have been a higher priority. We were told you guys had two unconscious victims and that ours were not serious."

"Yours were walking wounded," I tell him. "We had the two trapped in the vehicle who were unconscious on fire's arrival. They were reds as far as we knew. The ones you took were walking and talking. Those are greens and greens go last."

"Hey, I'm just letting you know, he was more critical," he tells me again, attempting to walk off.

"You're wrong. I checked them myself," I say back to the medic, stopping him. "They both had good mental status and were standing upright with good radial pulses. He might have ended up being the most injured, but he did not need to be transported first. The unconscious girls go first."

"I would have taken the boy first with that injury."

"I still wouldn't change a thing I did," I tell him.

He didn't agree, and he didn't have to. I could have kept arguing, but it wasn't going to change his mind. His decisions were based on facts gathered after the fact. He could review the game day footage all he wanted from the comfort of the training room, but I was the one who had to live the experience of being the first medic on scene and not having any information. I was the one who had to sort out the facts and make a quick and accurate decision based off the knowledge I obtained. And, I was the one who has to live with the results. I was confident in my choice and nothing was going to change that.

Nightmares

Working twenty-four hour shifts had taken its toll on me. Not only was it affecting my family life but it was destroying me mentally. The 911 system was busy enough, but working for an ambulance service meant you also had transfers between facilities during the downtime. It was an endless struggle which resulted in many sleepless nights.

On a normal work week, we reached seventy two hours on the clock. Time at home was spent recovering in preparation for the next shift. It became impossible to maintain any quality family life working in a busy system. Work was affecting home, but I had responsibilities. It was that same work that provided food for my family. I cared more about my wife and kids than my job, but I didn't know any other way to support my loved ones. Work continued to keep me in a slumber at home and kept me returning, only to repeat the cycle.

The effects of sleep deprivation accumulated. I began having strange dreams which only became worse as I kept starving my body of necessary rest. The dreams started as any normal one would. Within them were family members and people I interacted with the most. As peaceful as they started, they would quickly turn to periods of rage. Either my wife, brother or my dad would start screaming at me for no apparent reason. I had never seen them this furious before. At the top of their lungs, they would vent their frustration and displeasure at me. It made me feel unloved. I would cower down and remain silent. I only wanted the screaming to stop.

The dreams progressed to episodes of me lying in bed, unsure if I was actually asleep or not. The room was dark, but I could still see familiar surroundings. There were decorations on the wall and my wife lay by my side sleeping. I could see the TV in our room and items we had on our nightstand. I wondered why I was still awake. I was so tired and needed to get sleep before the next shift.

As I was looking around, an evil spirit entered the bedroom. It kept circling around and would envelope me with a feeling of hatred and anger. The spirit would not speak. Its message was telepathically delivered through its presence. I felt frozen. I would try to lift my head but I couldn't. I tried to open my eyes but they were forced shut. Finally, my mind would realize it was only a dream and I would snap back to reality.

Many of the dreams involved spiritual beings. Most were perceived as wicked due to the feelings which encompassed them. Others were present but their intentions were uncertain. They only brought fear of the unknown.

I was in my house playing with our kids who were running throughout, laughing and having a good time. I was happy to be home with my wife. It had been such a long week, but these were the moments I looked forward to. Suddenly, we were made aware that some sort of spirit was present throughout our home. There was no physical manifestation, just an unexplainable energy. It did not carry a sensation of love or hatred; it was neutral.

All of the lights were on throughout the house as they usually were just after dusk. The spirit's presence caused lights to flicker and burn out in the room where it was present. I tried to turn the lights back on, but flipping the switch was useless. I could feel a heaviness in the room coming from the ceiling and pouring down onto my body. As soon as that feeling left, the lights came back on. As I looked down the hallway, lights sequentially turned off and on as the spirit moved throughout our living space.

Each night, the dreams continued. My shifts ended in the morning where I would come home to an empty house. Exhausted from the endless night before, it didn't take long to begin falling asleep.

I started becoming overly aware of the process. The more I drifted off, the heavier my body became and the less responsive my senses were. The road noise outside my bedroom window would drift away as my mind shut out the external stimuli and allowed my body to rest. I was still awake, only experiencing the transition into sleep.

As the sounds of the world went away, I would begin to hear voices. They were muffled, but speaking constantly. It sounded like a group of people all chatting at once in a large room, and I was in the center. The further I progressed into the sleep cycle, the deeper I would get drawn in toward the voices. My body became heavier and the voices became louder. I did not like the feeling. I was afraid of what would happen if I got too far. Part of my mind was telling me that I was falling asleep and I needed to relax. The other half was screaming for me to wake up!

I could not withdrawal myself from the realm I was experiencing. Regardless of my efforts, I continued to be drawn toward their voices. They magnified and appeared to be multiplying. My body became heavier and heavier. Finally, I panicked, using every effort to escape. My mind convulsed as I suddenly withdrew from the terror. It felt like a seizure in my head, but in a snap, the voices were gone.

After a gasp of air, I sat bolt upright in my bed with my eyes open and my heart racing. Looking around the room, I was alone.

There was no resisting sleep. As much as I did not want to return to that world, it was inevitably going to happen. And so the nightmares continued.

The Real World

Lack of sleep, long hours, and low acuity responses were a disastrous formula. It limited reasoning, destroyed empathy, and ultimately led to a state of indifference. I felt that this response was an indicator that I wasn't cut out for the field. Many others were doing the same job and appeared to be handling the effects without issue. But, I kept pushing on, refusing to let anything stop me from doing what I loved to do. I figured I could overcome the issue with perseverance. Unaware of the true consequences, its effects slowly ingrained my life.

"Respond to the corner of 6th and MLK for a patient having chest pain," dispatch toned out our unit. Being stationed downtown had its ups and downs. We were one of the busiest units in the city which gave us more opportunity to run sick patients although the majority of the people who called for help did not need an ambulance. After running on countless complaints of nausea and vomiting, this report gave us a sigh of relief. Finally, we might have the chance to do what we were here to do.

With lights and sirens, we immediately headed off. We arrived to the reported intersection to find a woman sitting down at a bus stop bench clutching her chest with her right hand. She constantly rocked her body back and forth moaning in pain and seemed desperate for medical intervention.

"What's going on, ma'am?" I ask the anxious woman.

"I'm..." She pauses to catch her breath. "I'm having pain in my chest. It just started and it's really bad," she tells me.

"Is it just in your chest or do you feel any pain or discomfort anywhere else?"

"It's going down my left arm and into my jaw," she says.

I look at my partner. We both knew those were telltale symptoms of a heart attack, although the signs the woman couldn't control eased our worry about her severity. Her skin color was pink showing good perfusion of oxygenated blood throughout her body. Her blood pressure, heart rate, and other vital signs came back relatively normal. Either way, we had to investigate further and prepare for the worst.

"Let's give her three twenty four of aspirin and get a twelve lead," I tell my partner.

We move the patient to the comfort and privacy of our ambulance to perform the procedure. There was no need exposing this poor woman in public. Behind closed doors, I begin hooking her up to the cardiac monitor to obtain a detailed view of her heart's electrical activity.

The EKG comes back normal.

"Are you still having that pain in your chest and arm?" I reconfirm.

"Yes, it's really bad. Do you have something you can give me to make it go away?"

"I do," I tell her. "I'm going to spray this medicine under your tongue. Hopefully this will help."

I run a few rounds of sublingual nitroglycerine and prepare to transport the woman.

"We're going to take you to the hospital. It will be a quick trip down the road to the cardiac center..."

"No, I don't want to go there!" I get cut off. "Can you take me somewhere else?"

"Why?" I ask, confused.

"I had a bad experience there once," she tells me. "My friend almost died there and I don't trust the doctors. They almost killed her."

Immediately, déjà vu hit. This wasn't the first time I had heard this type of story. I had another patient tell me a similar situation where the doctors refused to care for their friend and they almost died as a result. Although the accusation was against a different facility, the motive I picked up behind the story was becoming awfully familiar.

"These are the best doctors in the area. I'm sorry to hear your friend had a bad experience but if you are having a heart attack that's where you are going to have the best chance at recovering."

With the patient's reported symptoms, I couldn't justify taking her to a less-capable facility. I had a duty to uphold, so we began transporting regardless.

As we neared the hospital campus, the patient insists, "It's still not working! The pain is really bad. I don't think it's my heart. It hurts, like in my ribs. You know, when I take a deep breath. Can you give me something else?"

"We're pulling into the hospital right now," I let her know. "These guys will take great care of you. I'll let the nurses know about your pain and that the nitro didn't work, okay?"

I drop the woman off, write my report in the lounge, and after a short snack break we get back in service.

We barely clear a few city blocks, heading back to our station, when the radio lights up again. "Respond to a chest pain, at the corner of..." the dispatcher reports, continuing to read off the address.

"That's the hospital! Well, the parking lot at least. That's right across the street!" I say.

"No way," my partner responds. "You think that's our last patient?"

"Better not be!" I say, pumping myself up over the hypothetical situation. "I swear she kept trying to get drugs off of me. I don't want to say she is full of shit if she was actually hurting, but there were some weird comments that came out that made me think otherwise."

"I think she was full of shit," my partner says bluntly. "She looked like a fucking druggie."

"Yeah, but they could have real problems too. I mean, you never know." I tried to stay optimistic. "It's just, when you're more worried about what hospital I'm taking you to and keep asking for something stronger for the pain, I can't help but think you're a seeker."

We flip around in the middle of the intersection, cutting off oncoming vehicles yielding to our lights and sirens. After a couple quick blocks of responding, we arrive on scene directly across the street from the hospital we had just left.

The fire department had just arrived and was already asking the patient questions. From far away, we could see a woman dramatically explaining her situation to the engine company. Her right hand was grasping her chest and her left arm was flailing around as she spoke. I walked up with a dead stare towards the woman's face, trying to identify her. I needed to know if she was our last patient or not.

As we approach with the gurney and medical bag, the woman quickly stares down at the ground. She begins covering her face with her hands as she continues explaining her story to the crew, now with less animation. It became obvious she was hiding from us.

I walked up hard to the circle of responders standing on the sidewalk and set my bag down.

"Let me guess, she's in her forties, chest pain radiating down the left arm and the hospital wouldn't do anything for her?" I say to the crew before they could give me a handoff report. They look at me confused by my attitude.

"Do you have your monitor?" the Lieutenant asks me.

"Yeah, but I'm not doing that again," I tell them. "Ma'am!" I shout to the patient. "Look at me. Take your hands off your face and look up at me right now!" She barely exposes her face as she raises her chin in my direction.

It's her.

"Yeah, I know it's you. Remember us? We just transported you five minutes ago to this hospital."

"You guys just transported her?" the Lieutenant asks.

"Yeah, she said she was having chest pain but didn't want to go here because of a bad experience in the past. Then she kept bugging me about giving her something stronger for the pain."

"Alright, I see," the Lieutenant responds. "So, what do you want from us now?" he asks the patient.

"I just need to go to another hospital. The doctors here refused to see me and they were mean to me. They told me to get out."

"Will you guys take her to another hospital?" the Lieutenant asks me, attempting to settle the matter. "Maybe that will make her happy so she stops calling."

"No!" I say adamantly. "If she wants to go we're going to the closest hospital and that's here. I will walk her back into the ER. I'm not playing her games. We're not going hospital shopping today!"

"Why don't you want to get checked in here?" the Lieutenant asks the patient.

"I told you. They refused to check me in. The doctor said I was banned from this hospital and he refused to see me. And, now I'm having chest pain and they won't let me in."

"No, that didn't happen," I cut her off.

"Are you saying I'm lying?" she asks sharply.

"Okay, in the real world, that doesn't happen. These guys hold pretty prestigious positions and worked nearly a decade to earn their titles. Do you really expect me to believe they are going to risk throwing it all away just to refuse to see you? No."

"I'm not going there!" she demands.

"We're not taking you anywhere else," I tell her.

"Fine. Then I will just keep calling!"

The comment had me speechless. She had gained the upper hand. I didn't know how to respond. She was right. She had power over us. She had the power to make my day miserable, and she knew it. Fortunately, the Lieutenant was quick to respond.

"How about we call the police here to help you make a decision then. Would you like to speak to one of our officers?"

"Fine! I'll go," she finally gives in. She grabs her bags and begins walking on her own toward the emergency department across the street. I catch up and escort the woman. During our walk, I decide to have a quiet conversation between the two of us.

"What are you looking for? What are you trying to get from me?" I ask.

She remains silent.

"Are you looking for drugs? Looking for attention? What is it?"

Still, she remains silent.

I sigh. "Look, you can keep calling 911 if you want. But, if you call in my district, I'm going to show up. I'm going to keep showing up every time you call. And I'm going to remember your face. I know you and I'm going to tell others about you. And we're not going to put up with your bullshit. You'll never get drugs off of me or anyone of us out here."

We walk in through the triage doors.

"You're back again," the woman at the registration desk says, looking surprised.

I give a quick report to the triage nurse and began walking away.

"Have a great day, ma'am."

SIXTH SENSE

Don't ever let patients affect you. The words from my instructors were more relevant than they ever had been before. The good old days of being a naive rookie blind to the situations we were actually involved with were over. This is what they had been talking about.

The advice had me prepared to deflect a patient's anger or acts of aggression, most of which were brought on as a result of their actual illness, so it never bothered me. A hypoxic patient calling me a piece of shit due to his lack of oxygen or a hypoglycemic patient getting combative due to a low blood sugar was expected in this field. What got me fired up was when patients, day after day, thought they could insult my intelligence and deceive me into giving them drugs.

I tried not to let the last patient dictate my attitude for the next. I would start fresh with each new contact, happy and eager to help, but usually end up bitter and feeling resentment towards the end. It was a constant cycle of hope and despair.

Just before all hope was gone, a call would come in that would completely turn the tables. It would erase every bad experience from the previous stretch and restore my passion once again.

We got called for a man who fell. We arrive on scene to find a heavy-set man in his forties lying on the floor of a fast-food restaurant lobby.

"Hey, man, what happened?" I begin my assessment.

"These damn kids didn't have any wet floor signs out and I slipped and fell trying to walk up to the counter."

I take a look around the area, spotting multiple bright colored warning signs.

"There's three wet floor signs I can see right around us..."

"Well, they put them there after I fell!" the patient cuts in.

This wasn't my problem. I was off track and needed to redirect the flow of this call.

"So you fell? Where are you hurting?" I ask.

"My neck and back. I fell backwards and hit my head on the ground."

"Alright, let me check you out."

Through the tossing and turning in pain, I assess his body for signs of trauma. Pushing on the man's spine elicited a loud scream and more jerking around. Although there was no bruising or bleeding, we immobilized his body to a backboard as a precaution.

As we were packaging the patient, one of the restaurant employees timidly interrupts.

"Umm, guys. He didn't fall and we had wet floor signs out before he even came in."

"What do you mean he didn't fall?" my partner asks. "What did you guys see?"

"He kind of made a scene and threw himself on the ground," the worker tells us, with a few others behind her shaking their heads in agreement.

"Did he hit his head?" my partner asks.

"No, he caught himself with his hands before hitting the ground. Then he rolled around screaming and yelling at us to call 911."

"That's a fucking lie!" the patient responds. "My head hurts so bad. I can't believe they didn't even have warning signs out. That's messed up. I hit my head so hard I passed out and they're going to lie to your face and say it was my fault. You guys need to take me to the hospital right now!"

My sympathy for this person was fading fast. I sided with the employees. There were no physical injuries. He had an overdramatic response to pain on my assessment of his neck and back. But most of all, he was more concerned there were no wet floor signs present than he was about his injuries.

In the ambulance, the patient continues his rant.

"They're going to pay for this. My neck could have been broken. And I have a splitting headache. Is there anything you can give me for the pain?"

Once again, he was sounding like the rest of them.

"I can't give you anything. If you have a brain bleed going on, that medicine will make it worse. Just hang in there, buddy. We're almost to the hospital," I reassure him.

"How long until we get there?" he asks.

"Maybe another five minutes," I tell him.

"And they will give me pain medicine there?"

"I can't tell you what they will or won't do there. The nurses and doctor will examine you and make a decision."

For the next couple minutes the patient lay flat on the backboard quietly. After establishing an IV, I started typing my report and preparing for the handoff with the emergency department.

Suddenly, the patient's body starts violently convulsing. His arms and legs uncontrollably shake and his eyes are closed. Obviously, my judgment was off. He did fall. He did hit his head. And, his condition had now deteriorated.

"Shit! He's seizing. Step it up priority!" I yell to my EMT driving.

Without hesitation, I unlock the narcotics cabinet and reach for an anticonvulsant to stop the seizure.

Valium.

I rip the tag off the drug box and begin prepping for administration. While quickly confirming the dose and concentration on the vial, something grabbed my attention causing me to glance at the patient.

He was looking right at me.

Through the convulsions and supposed lack of mentation, the patient had locked eyes with me. This could only happen in a conscious state of mind.

I had experienced this instinct before. When I was younger, my friends and I were addicted to paintballing. One day, we were matched up against a small group of Army veterans. Although we out-gunned our opponent, we were no match for their level of skill. Except for one instance.

In this instance, I learned more about the human body's capability than ever before. I was standing guard at a sandbag bunker. The vet had advanced on my position undetected, crawling with his camouflaged body tight to the ground. Inch by inch, he progressed on my position in an attempt to ambush me.

Recalling the story after the game, he said, "I knew better than to look you in the eyes. As soon as I looked at you, you turned right toward me and shot me!"

I had no idea he was there. The only thing that made me victorious that day was my instinct. It was the same instinct which showed me the truth behind my current patient's attempt.

"Hey!" I call him out. "I saw you. You looked at me!" I tell him. I was in disbelief. I was ready to push a heavy dose of benzodiazepines into his system. I locked the drugs back up to secure them.

"This dude is faking!" I shout to the EMT.

"You still want me to go priority?" he asks.

"Yeah, you might as well. We're almost there."

I turn my attention back to the patient.

"Hey! Open your eyes. I'm not giving you shit now. Open your eyes and stop faking!"

He doesn't stop.

I change my tone, telling him softly, "Hey, you screwed up. You almost got it, but not this time. You shouldn't have looked at me."

He keeps convulsing. Part of me wondered if I was wrong. I was not about to withhold a necessary medicine to someone in need; someone whose life depended on it. I began doubting myself. I hated that I was in this predicament.

Did I see what I thought I saw? What if I was wrong? What if he suffers because I was afraid of ruining my pride?

I give it another shot. Digging my knuckles deep into his sternum, I try to inflict a dose of pain to get him to respond.

Still nothing.

I debate inside as we rush toward the hospital. I clearly remember his face. His eyes were tracking mine. He quickly looked away once we made eye contact. There was no mistake. He was a professional. He wanted drugs and this is how he was going to get them. I knew what I saw.

Okay. One last shot, I think to myself. *If this doesn't work, he's getting the Valium. He would deserve it at that point even if he is faking.*

I hold the man's face still and open his eye lid. The man stares straight up. His pupil remains still. With the index finger of my right hand, I reach in and gently tap his eye.

The guy jerks his head away, breathing heavy from the shock he just experienced.

"What the fuck, man! What the fuck was that!" he shouts irately.

"That?" I respond. "That is what happens when you fake a fucking seizure in my ambulance."

"God damnit, man!"

TOUGH GUYS

Having a good partner on shift was imperative. The days were long enough as they were. Worst, was to drag out an already extensive period of time with someone who carried a negative attitude. It was beneficial having an EMT with skill in patient care, but when it came down to it I would rather have a partner with an amusing personality.

In an attempt to improve my sleep situation, I decided to take a new shift which had just opened. By some miracle, I was able to not only find the hours which worked better for my life, but also the best work partner I could ask for.

One of the first calls we ran was on a patient who had left the bar and was stumbling down the street. He had fallen and hit his head causing bystanders to call 911. Even with some resistance in cooperation, we were able to get the guy loaded for transport.

The patient was covered with tattoos. He talked tough and tried to tell us how things were going to be. Skyler and I quickly put an end to his attitude and let him know who was really in charge. We liked to be laid back and have a good time on the rig, but when it came down to it no one else was going to run our show.

The man was intoxicated and had a head injury. There was no question he needed an IV. Effects of alcohol could mask critical symptoms in a trauma patient. Even though we were certain his injuries would not be life-threatening, it was our job to prepare for the worst case.

I take a look at the man's arm. Within his sleeve are various devilish figures and prison-related insignia.

"Let me see your arm, I'm going to give you an IV," I explain to him.

His defiant attitude continues.

"I'll kick your fucking ass if you try! Fuck you! Get away from me."

I pause and take a deep breath before I respond. We had achieved the upper hand earlier and gaining enough cooperation to get the guy in our rig. His attitude had settled down until he saw the large needle I was about to put in him. I decide to change the game plan and ask for cooperation instead of demanding it. I knew where we would end up if I didn't back down from the latter.

"Hey, man, you hit your head. I'm going to have to get a line in you."

"You get close to me with that needle and I'll fucking kill you."

"What's wrong? Why don't you want an IV?"

"That shit hurts! I don't need it."

"Oh, come on, man, it's not *that* bad. It's not any worse than those tattoos you have."

He still does not budge.

"Alright, how about this? I'll make it quick. I'll only poke you once. That's all I'll need. If I don't get it, then I'll leave it for the hospital. Deal?"

He continues to pull his arm away.

"Get the fuck away from me with that needle." The look in his face is pure hatred. I still have to get this IV. I try and reason with him one last time before changing plans.

"Look, man, you've been drinking a lot tonight, right?"

He shakes his head, yes.

"Alcohol thins your blood. If you have a bleed going on in your head, this thing will save your life," I say as I show him the long needle. It sounded better in my head before the words came out. The show was a bit melodramatic, but I was also running out of options while keeping it civil.

The response I got was not at all what I expected.

"It'll save my life?" he asks. The anger had left and his eyes started to tear up.

I decided to go with it.

"Uh... yeah. If I can get you an IV it *will* save your life." The cheesy made-for-TV medic voice kicked in as I tried to put on a show for my partner while he drove.

"You're going to save my life?" he responds.

"Yep. Now, let's get this IV in, okay."

The patient cooperates and I get the IV in on the first try.

On our way to the hospital, the patient breaks down and starts crying. "Man, did you really save my life?" The game was over in my mind. I got what I wanted. But to him, it was still real.

"You're doing fine, buddy. Just hang tight, alright. We'll be at the hospital shortly."

"You saved my life, man, that's real shit!"

I smile at the transformation he made. My partner starts cracking up from the front seat.

"I want to shake your hand," he continues. He extends up a hand from up the backboard and I shake it.

It's a wonderful sight arriving at the hospital, knowing I can offload this highly-emotional patient. We sit in the hallway waiting for registration as the patient lays on the backboard, face up toward the ceiling and unable to move his neck from the rigid cervical collar that has been applied.

I position myself at the foot end of the gurney to avoid any further interaction with the guy.

He looks up at my partner positioned at the head and asks, "Where is he? I need to shake his hand."

"Who?" Skyler asks. "My partner?"

"Yeah. What's his name? I need to know his name," he shouts dramatically.

I look back. *You better keep your mouth shut,* I tell him through my stare.

My partner looks back at me with a smirk. "Dave. His name is Dave."

You fucker! I shake my head at him.

"Dave!' the patient shouts. "Dave! Get over here!"

God damnit! I think, smiling now.

People in the ER start staring at me as I obviously avoid my patient. I reluctantly walk over to the head of the gurney to make an appearance. "Dave. Are you there?" he asks. He tries to turn his head in my direction, but it is taped town to the board and can't move.

"Yeah, I'm here."

"I can't see you, brother."

"That's 'cause you're strapped to a board, dude."

"Dave..." He pauses. "Look me in the eye, man!"

"Yeah, I can't really look you in the eyes..." I say, sarcastically. His eyes move to the deep peripheries to try and catch a glimpse of my face.

He reaches his arm out.

"Hold my hand, fool." He extends his arm out further. Embarrassment from the situation starts to really set in as I can feel everyone in the ER watching the show unfold. I look at my partner and he is cracking up, unable to hold quiet any longer.

I grab his hand and attempt to give him another quick shake, but he pulls me in closer.
"You saved my life, brother."
The nurses laugh amongst each other and take their sweet time finding us a room.

THAT'S ALREADY BEEN DONE

I'm not sure when the point of desensitization kicked in exactly. Maybe it was an effect over years of experiencing death and misery. Although I tried to detach from the emotion of those calls, it kept creeping back months later. Ultimately though, I believe my numbness to human concern came from the system abusers. Drugs caused most of the issues which led to people needing an ambulance. They were either on them, wanted them, or had some problem caused by them.

  I had become heartless from overexposure. It was all I was experiencing every day. Although I wasn't thrilled about the attitude I was adapting, my insensitivity and crude humor fit right in to the culture of the workplace. The change was inevitable with the experiences we faced. It allowed you to cope with the frustration of a broken system.

Between running 911 calls, our unit was sent to a hospital to transfer a schizophrenic patient to a long-term mental health facility. I saw the illness differently than others in the profession. Through my corrupt vision, I saw that most of these cases involved prior use of meth, LSD, or other hardcore substances. It was this drug-induced state which allowed evil into their hearts resulting in what we labeled psychosis.

Our patient had come into the hospital with delusions and homicidal thoughts. The transfer to the gurney went effortlessly. Immediately, we placed him in restraints. He didn't resist. He continued to carry on a conversation with himself consisting of meaningless mixtures of random phrases.

"Alright," I begin. "We are going to take you to a metal health facility, and..."

His conversation stops as he cuts me off. "I've been there before."

"Okay, well we're going back, then," I tell him. "How did you get to the hospital today?"

"The hospital!" he replies angrily. "I am going to fucking kill every one of those mother fuckers there!"

"Whoa?" I say, with a little laugh. The reply wasn't too far off from expected based on his history of having homicidal thoughts, but it caught me off guard. Now my interest was piqued. These were the stories that made my day.

"So, you're not a fan of the hospital?"

"I am going to get a gun and shoot every one of those fucking nurses in there!"

I cut him off, "Wait! You can't do that!"

He doesn't listen.

"I'm going to kill everyone in there! I'm going to shoot them all!"

"You can't do that!" I interrupt.

"Why not!" he questions me angrily.

"Because, that's already been done before," I tell him. "Remember Columbine? Two kids came in with guns and shot up a school. You got to do something bigger than that. Something unique."

"Hmm..." he ponders the thought for a bit. "You're right." He pauses for a few moments in silence. Then the next genius plan pops into his head.

"Alright, I'm going to get a plane and crash it into the hospital and kill all those mother fuckers..."

I cut him off again, "No, no, no, you can't do that!"

"Why the hell not?" He is getting irritated now.

"Remember 9/11? Terrorists hijacked planes and crashed them into the World Trade Center. That's already been done, too. You need to think of something else. Something no one has ever done before."

We spent the remainder of the transport in silence. I wrote my report and the patient attempted to think of the next creative way to kill everyone at the hospital.

Careful What You Wish For

Taking the emotion out of patient encounters is what made life manageable on the ambulance. It was difficult to do, but necessary to carry out the orders of the medical system or the wishes of a patient.

Crude humor often resulted. Somehow it made reality a little more tolerable. Our insensitive jokes were kept in private amongst us. They served more as a coping mechanism to get us through the day, although most of us wouldn't want to admit it. Doing so would show weakness. The weak didn't make it in this field.

We pulled into a local hospital for one of our scheduled facility transports. The woman was a vegetable. She couldn't move. She couldn't speak. She couldn't even blink her eyes. She was kept alive artificially through a feeding tube, dialysis treatments, and a ventilator. She was the result of the medical system's efforts which were enough to save her life but not enough to provide quality or prevent suffering.

It was difficulty watching the family cling to any hope of improvement. We knew better. We didn't see hope. We saw a poor woman in agony day after day.

We wheel our gurney in past the EMS lounge on our way to pick up the patient.

"Who are you guys here for?" one of the other crews asks.

We tell them.

"Man, she's still alive?" they sound surprised. Some of us were counting down the days.

"Dude, I swear. I think I'm just going to get a pillow and put her out of her misery," I joke with the crew. "I don't know. She just stopped breathing," I mimic the situation sarcastically. "She would want me to do it. If she could, she would probably grab the damn pillow out of my hands and do it herself!"

The crew stood there with a smirk on their faces.

"I hope she doesn't die on you because I'm going to think you guys actually did that if she does," they tell me.

"I'm just messing around," I say. "I feel bad for her. I just hope the flu or something takes her out so she doesn't have to suffer anymore."

We loaded the patient, padding every rail and bar on our gurney with extra pillows from the linen closet. I put a blanket on her and positioned her head to help ease her breathing for the ride. We ended up dropping the patient off with an uneventful transport.

Months later, we get sent out to the same hospital for a routine transfer. My partner reads the information on his pager.

"Seriously!" he shouts. We recognized the name immediately. "I wish she would just die already!"

As much as we hated the situation, we had no control over it. We were there to provide care and be as compassionate as possible. We grabbed extra pillows from the linen closet as we progressed towards her bed. As we wheeled the stretcher through the doors of the dialysis center, we heard the intercom announce, "Code blue, dialysis, rapid response team, now."

"You don't think that's our patient?" I ask my partner. He looks shocked. With a nervous look, he tries to shrug it off.

We enter the doors. There's a commotion around the bed. The same bed we always pick up from. But, the crowd of medical personnel and onlookers is thick and we can't see who the victim is. As the rapid response team pushes through the crowd, we get a glimpse of the patient's face.

It's her.

"I don't think she's going anywhere," I say quietly to my partner, as we sit amongst the onlookers watching the hospital personnel perform. Moments later, the rush ends. The woman is as motionless as she had been while she was living. This time, a sheet gets drawn across her.

Reality was harsh. We walk back to our rig with an empty gurney. My partner says nothing. As we get in, I look at him and say, "You know you killed her, right?"

He laughs a little and looks at me shocked. "What?" he says, chuckling nervously. "No I didn't!"

"Yes you did. You said I hope she dies, and now look what happened. She's dead! You killed her!" I am smiling as I speak to him.

"Fuck, dude! I didn't mean it. I mean, I really didn't want her dead. I just didn't want to do the transport again. I hate having to see that." He sat there, thinking about the situation. "Man, I'm never saying that again."

"You know you're going to hell, right?" I tell him, laughing. He just shakes his head in disbelief. As much as we felt the woman was suffering, it was still difficult watching her die. I just hoped she was in a better place; somewhere more peaceful and comfortable than she had spent the last year of her life.

ONE DAY LATER

There are moments in life where you feel you were put in a certain place and time for a reason. You don't know it until the significance of the moment reveals itself. Every day we cross paths with others and have the opportunity to make a difference in their life, even in a small way. When presented with this opportunity, some people take action and know they made a difference. Some are indifferent and move on with their business. Others fail to act and feel regret once the opportunity passes.

The field had numbed me to the misery others faced. I developed an insensitive, uncaring personality. I was getting burned out by the system. The repeated exposure to negativity wore on me. It changed me from the happy, energetic individual I once was to one of gloom and depression. Maybe it was an accumulation of the emergency scenes I had been exposing myself to. Maybe it was a result of how I had been treating those who I crossed paths with.

Searching for answers to my despair, I found a passage which put many things into perspective. *We meet simply another version of ourselves every day.* I knew I needed to change but I didn't know how. Every time I thought I made progress, I would be exposed to one more form of evil. It was causing me to lose faith in mankind.

The call came out around midnight. We were sent out non-emergent to evaluate a reported dizzy two year old a few miles from our station. The dispatch information seemed odd, but it wouldn't be the first time we were sent on a 911 call for a ridiculous complaint. We pulled up to the scene and situated ourselves behind the fire engine.

At the front porch, the firefighters were accompanying a young woman who was holding her child.

"What's going on with the kid," I ask the Lieutenant.

"The mom says he's feeling dizzy. But, she's also complaining of dizziness and nausea herself."

"They're all feeling dizzy?" I confirm. Suddenly the call took a turn. Maybe it was a legitimate complaint. "Any chance of carbon monoxide?"

"She said their furnace was out and they have been using space heaters to heat the place. I sent one of my guys in to check it out."

"Alright. Well, let's get to the ambulance and get some fresh air," I direct the mother.

The fact we were dispatched for a dizzy two year old kept pressing at me. I needed more information. Something didn't seem right. *How would she know her two year old was dizzy? A two year old wouldn't know how to explain such a symptom.* As we walked to the rig, I question the mom further.

"How long ago did you begin feeling dizzy?"

"I started feeling dizzy when I walked into my son's bedroom," she responds.

"And he's feeling dizzy too?"

"Yeah."

"Where were you inside the house?"

"In the living room."

"What was your son doing when you walked in?" I ask, wondering if the source of the dizziness was originating in his bedroom.

"He was sleeping." That made sense. It was midnight.

"How long had he been sleeping?"

"I put him to bed a couple hours ago. But, he was in a deeper sleep than normal."

Huh? I help the woman and her child into the back of the ambulance. With better lighting, I can see that neither have flushed skin, a sign of carbon monoxide poisoning. They both look relaxed. The kid looks like he wants to go back to sleep.

"So, your son had been sleeping for hours and you were awake in the living room. What made you go in his room?"

"I just knew something was wrong. It was a motherly instinct."

"How do you know he's dizzy?" I question further, trying to uncover something. The story wasn't adding up. There was a piece I was still missing. She just looked at me with a blank stare on her face.

"He's two. Was he was able to tell you he was dizzy?" I interrogate her.

"I figured he was dizzy because I was," she tells me.

"So, was your son complaining of anything?"

"No."

"What made you call 911?"

"You know this neighborhood. There are strange people everywhere. They look in his windows and I don't know if the doors are locked and I was scared."

Finally, the piece I was missing became apparent. It explained everything.

This is a psych call. The real patient is the mother.

I continued to question her about her history which revealed that she had been hearing voices in her head. The unveiled history of auditory hallucinations only confirmed my suspicions.

I complete the assessment on the mother and move on to check out the child. He was wrapped in a blanket and sleeping now. I gently unwrap the blanket to examine further. He was wearing only a diaper, but looked clean and healthy for the most part. Moving down further, I notice the soles of his feet are completely black from the amount of dirt buildup.

Watching my assessment, the mom tells me, "Oh, he didn't get his bath today. I'm so embarrassed. He's not even dressed. He is supposed to get a bath tomorrow," she assures me.

"That's okay," I tell her. It looked nasty, but the rest of his body was clean and healthy. *He had probably been running around on dirty floors*, I figured.

"You guys both look like you're doing fine right now. Your vital signs are normal and your son looks comfortable. I'm not seeing any signs of carbon monoxide poisoning which could cause you guys to get dizzy. I think it may have something to do with the voices you are hearing. What do you think?"

"Well, maybe. I've been doing so good," she says.

The firefighters returned from examining the house and meet me at the ambulance. I update them on the psychiatric history so we are all on the same page. The Lieutenant steps in the back of the rig and sits down next to the mother.

"What are all of those pills in the sink?" he asks.

Pills? I wonder. Again, the call takes another strange route.

"Those are just ibuprofen," the mother says defensively.

"How did they get in the sink?"

"He poured out the bottle, but he didn't take any. I swear!" she insists.

"I think it is best if we take you and your son to the hospital," the Lieutenant continues. "I know you called 911 because you were concerned about your son, so we will check him into the children's hospital."

"We'll take you in to get evaluated while your son is getting checked out next door, okay," I tell the mom. She agrees and sits back cooperatively. During the transport, the woman remains quiet and stares at the floor.

"Is everything still alright with you?" I ask. "Are you feeling dizzy again?"

"No, I feel kind of stupid now. I don't think we need to go to the hospital."

I could tell she truly cared for her son's wellbeing, but it was evident she needed help. She needed treatment so she could be the best mom possible for her little one.

"You shouldn't feel stupid," I tell her. "Something happened in there that wasn't normal, right?"

She shakes her head slightly, agreeing.

"Now, we don't know why you guys started feeling dizzy but that is something we can find out at the hospital."

I feed into her perceived reality of the situation to gain cooperation. The child needed to be evaluated with the newly discovered possibility of an overdose. The mother needed a mental health evaluation before I felt comfortable with her being released to care for her child. I proceeded to call the hospital which would be accepting the mother to give them a heads up of our arrival.

"We have a woman complaining of dizziness but is currently asymptomatic. Apparently she states she had a motherly instinct that her two year old son was also dizzy so we're bringing him in too."

"So, you're bringing the kid to the children's side?" the nurse confirms.

"That's affirmative. We'll see you in five."

"Okay, just bring them both to triage," I am told.

I hang up the phone and immediately give the children's hospital a call.

"Hi, we're bringing you guys a two year old male for dizziness and to rule out a possible overdose. We also have his mother as a patient that will be seen for a psych eval. I already called report on the mom and we were told to bring both to triage."

"Okay, we'll see you guys in triage."

When we arrive at the hospital, I have the mother step out of the side door first. Noticing his mother leaving, the child begins screaming and crying with his arms outstretched in her direction. We try to soothe him, but he only wants his mother. She wraps him in her arms, consoling him quickly.

We walk both patients to the triage area. Everything was going smoothly. Just as I was about to hand over care, the charge nurse puts a wrench in my plan.

"The child can't go back by himself. The mother has to accompany her child during the evaluation."

What the fuck are you doing? I wonder.

"No. She needs to be evaluated on the other side for psych," I insist. I had already explained all of this on the phone.

"She has to be with her child while he's being evaluated. We can't have kids here without their parents."

"She's a patient!" I argue, but they don't listen.

Frustration sets in as the situation slips out of my control. The charge nurse escorts the mom and child through the doors of the children's emergency department and I give report to the triage nurse.

I explain the dirty feet and the ibuprofen pills found in the sink. I tell her about the mother's hallucinations and how she had responded to my questions. I felt that she was in no condition to care for her child in her current state. The nurse assures me that they will refer the case to child protective services and get the mother a psychiatric workup. Feeling satisfied with their plan, I get a transfer of care signature for the child.

I track down the nurse who is supposed to accept care of the mother, but she will not accept report.

"You didn't give us a patient," she tells me.

I was not about to accept that. I had a plan and they fucked it up. I was not leaving the hospital until I had documented transfer of care of the mother also.

"I brought the mother in as a patient. The charge nurse decided to take her back with her child." My diligence pays off. I get sent back up front and the charge nurse agrees to sign my report.

The remainder of the evening went by uneventful. The next morning, I arrived early to my regular shift station. The day carried on like normal. A few hours into the shift, I get a call from the EMT I worked with the night before.

"Have you driven by that house where we picked up the kid and the mother last night?" he asks.

"No, why?"

"I drove by that address on my way into work and there was police tape and cop cars out front. You heard the story on the news, right?"

I stop to think. Suddenly my heart sank. I get a knot in my throat as I recall the story which had been aired all morning on the news.

'Mother *Says She Killed her 2-Year Old.*' The face of the woman and her child had been plastered all over television.

"Holy shit! That's that same lady?"

"I think so," he replies.

The news reported the mother called 911 stating she had just killed her son. She told authorities she crushed his head against the dresser multiple times and then smothered him with a pillow. The two-year olds body was found with blood on his face and he was not breathing. The mom had blood on her hands. She explained to investigators that voices in her head told her to kill him.

Later that day, a picture and name of the boy flash across the screen.

"That's the kid," I tell my partner. "I remember his name." I felt helpless. The image of the boy was stuck in my mind.

He was healthy. He was comforted by his mother. And she showed concern for him. How could she do this? I did everything I could to stop this from happening. I was the only thing in her way and somehow I failed.

I began second guessing my actions.

There must have been something I could have done. I should not have let that nurse take both of them back. I was worried about her slipping through the cracks and not being evaluated. I should have demanded she get seen right away. They didn't know her as well as I did. It took a while for me to see through her façade and find her true illness. I should have done something more. I was put there for a reason and I didn't pull through.

My mind raced for the rest of the day. I was full of regret and couldn't think straight. Memories from the call keep coming back. Guilt started to seep in. I knew there was only one way to drown the feeling.

Possessed

What if everything they said was real? What if it's not a chemical imbalance or disease process causing them to act the way they did? What would cause them to turn from loving and caring to homicidal? What could cause someone to want to kill their own child? What was controlling them?

Questions raced through my head that would not receive answers. I didn't understand it. If you listen to a person who is labeled schizophrenic, many of their words speak from a spiritual or religious nature. No one listens to them because the words coming out of their mouth don't coincide with the world as we know it. The answer is to lock them up in a psychiatric hospital and sedate them with medication. The problem goes away and we carry on with our normal lives.

Many mentally ill patients claimed to be demons or Lucifer himself who had taken over the body. I chalked it up to a fried brain from heavy drug use in the beginning, but the more I experienced similarities, the more I began wondering, What if everything they said was real? It became even more real months later. I wasn't ready for what I was about to experience.

 We got called out to an upstairs apartment for a woman in her fifties who had not been acting appropriately. The woman had refused to get out of bed for days and was making vulgar comments which scared the family even more.

 We arrived to the apartment and found the fire crew huddled inside a small back bedroom. They tell us that the patient has been acting strange for the past three days. Initially, her family thought she was sick, but today they knew something was majorly wrong.

 I take a peek in the bedroom and everything looked normal. The woman lay in bed insisting that she did not need to go to the hospital. Her son looked worried and tried to convince her to be seen. The fire crew remained insistent that the woman was mentally ill. Her vitals were normal, including a blood sugar and temperature.

 "You guys are thinking psych?" I confirm. "Is she alert and making sense?"

 "No, not at all!" They are persistent in the fact, although it was something I had not yet seen for myself.

 The Lieutenant warns me, "She doesn't want to go and will probably get violent if we try to take her."

 I say confidently, "I got something that will take care of that." I am not afraid of a fight, but this woman didn't look like a fighter. I was more worried about her family turning on us. Before I got too worked up over the comment, I needed to assess the patient myself.

 I began speaking to the woman.

 "What's your name?" I ask, without introducing myself. It was a bad habit I had formed to jump right in and figure out the problem rather than build rapport first.

 She tells me her name and we continue to carry on a normal conversation. Everyone else was adamant she was altered. I continue asking questions but am confused by her normal responses. Suddenly, the conversation strays and she begins speaking like the schizophrenic patients we normally see.

She no longer responds to my questioning.

"Ma'am, we're going to take you to the hospital," I tell her. "You might have an infection or something going on that is causing you to be confused." I wanted the family to understand we had no intention of being mean if it came to forcing her. To ensure their compliance, I needed to demonstrate that I cared for her wellbeing as much as they did.

"Now, I know you are confused and probably don't understand what I am telling you, but we need to get you to the hospital so you can feel better."

She actually responds, "I'm fine. I don't want to go anywhere."

Yeah, you really don't have a choice, I think to myself.

"Can you stand up and walk down with me to the gurney so we can get you the help you need?"

Seeing that my attempts are ineffective, the son steps in and attempts to persuade her. Knelt by the bedside, he says, "Mom, you need to go to the hospital so the doctors can make you better..."

The woman lurches forward and begins punching her son in the head.

He backs away, not even defending himself from the strikes. Looking up with a horrified look on his face, he leaves the room under the comfort of the remaining family members. I didn't even know what to say. The attack completely caught me off guard. I let him pass by and refocus my attention on the woman.

This person had loved and raised him. It was visible in his concern for her. Something caused her to lash out in anger. I was done asking politely. It was time to take her out the hard way.

"Get the restraints and a backboard," I tell my partner. He immediately turns around and heads down the stairway. I briefly step out of the room and ask the family members, "Does she have any history of psychotic disorders such as schizophrenia or bipolar?"

"No, never," they tell me.

"Is there any possibility she has been on drugs or alcohol?"

"No, she doesn't even drink."

"Has she been sick recently? Has she had a fever or been throwing up?"

"We thought she might not be feeling well because she has been in bed the last three days, but she hasn't been weak or vomiting or anything. She just refused to get out of bed. It's very weird. And then today, she started acting like this!"

I get my plan set with the Lieutenant. "Let's get all of the family out of here while we restrain her. This is going to get ugly." He agrees and starts directing everyone to leave the apartment. The family is cooperative in giving us the space we need.

There is no more reasoning with the patient. We enter the room with the force of five strong. There is no discussion. Blindsiding the woman, we each take an extremity while the fifth helps control the head. Quickly, restraints are applied to her arms and legs. Surprisingly, she does not fight back. She lays back and speaks calmly.

"You can't stop me," she says with a smirk on her face.

As we move her to the gurney, she identifies herself as the devil. She continues speaking of spirits and demons and other religious figures. She laughs as she talks. It becomes a mental game against us.

As we carry the woman down the stairs, she looks at each and every one of us while speaking in tongues. She becomes enraged as soon as we pass the family members standing outside.

"You fucks! You will all go to hell you fucking cowards!"

As we load her into the ambulance, the rage silences. My partner joins me in the back and closes the doors. The woman's eyes are closed. I try to talk to her but she doesn't budge. She won't look at me or respond to me. I try to force her eyes open but she resists.

"Open your eyes!" I demand, but she squints tighter.

We prepare for another set of vitals, but ultimately decide to leave her alone because the quiet atmosphere was actually quite nice. I would rather a peaceful ride to the hospital than screaming and shouting.

"Alright, let's go," I quietly tell my partner. As he begins to exit, the woman opens her eyes. She looks over and begins asking me questions. I don't feed in to her conversation. Instead, I try to pry information out of her.

"Did you take anything?" I ask her. "Any drugs?" She does not respond to my questioning and continues with her rant. It's useless. My partner goes up front and starts driving us to the hospital.

"I am Lucifer," the woman continues. "This woman will not get released. I control her..."

I ignore the talk for the most part and type up my report. I do not give her the satisfaction of letting her know I am listening. Suddenly something catches my attention.

"You know who I am, David..."

I stop my writing. The woman is staring right into my eyes. I didn't feel frightened. I was curious. I decided to confront her.

"What's my name?" I ask.

She doesn't respond to me and continues speaking in tongues.

"Hey!" I shout at her. "What did you call me? You just said my name. What's my name?"

I can't get her attention.

"How did you know my name?" I ask her calmly. I had not introduced myself to this woman.

I felt assured that I would be protected from whatever had just pried at me. I didn't know what it was and after the things she said, I really didn't want to find out. Something wanted to make its presence known to me. This time, it wasn't in a dream or a story on the news. This time it was close and personal.

Afterward, I ask my partner, "Did you call me by my name at all on that last call?"

He responds, "No, I don't think so."

"Did fire call me 'David' at all?"

"No," he responds, trying to recollect. 'Why?"

"The patient called me David. I didn't give her my name, though. I'm wondering how she knew it."

"Well, someone probably called you by your name on scene. I might have. I don't even remember," he tells me, shrugging it off.

"Maybe, but everyone calls me Stone."

He didn't understand and I didn't expect him to. He didn't experience it.

"I don't know, man, that's just weird," I tell him.

I spoke about the event to only three people: my wife, my mom and my brother. My wife thought the whole situation was eerie and didn't doubt the events. She was proud of me for being strong and prayed that I would stay safe.

My mom sat down with me and appeared very serious about the incident. She explained that she believes demons are out there but that God will keep us safe. She believes it is up to us to do good in the world and carry out God's plan.

My brother began telling me about books he had read on similar subjects where people had accounts of being possessed. What he said wasn't like 'The Exorcist' where they're throwing up green vomit and climbing on ceilings. He explained that the reports showed the affected person, or the voice inside, would say they were the devil but experts believe they are more of a demon. He also said that the possessed had revealed facts about a person that hadn't been disclosed openly.

I believe that my guardian angels protected me and continue watching over me. It was only through their power that I was able to remain fearless in the face of evil that exposed itself.

Primum Non Nocere

The words were painted on the wall of the education building. They were presented throughout the textbook. It was the first thing taught in EMT training.

'*Primum Non Nocere.*' The Latin phrase, First Do No Harm, was the foundation of our duty as emergency responders. It was the basis of our morals as people helping others. I based every decision in the field off of it.

We get dispatched with a neighboring volunteer fire department to a patient having trouble breathing. Their house was situated on a steep hill and access to the residence was further impeded with cars in the narrow driveway. At the top of the hill, we park the ambulance on the street and carry our equipment inside.

One look at the woman tells me that we will not be spending any more time on scene.

"Grab our gurney," I tell one of the volunteers. I immediately look to my partner and say, "Set me up a nebulizer and CPAP, we'll meet you back at the rig." The woman had been huffing on breathing treatments for the past few hours with no relief. She was almost beyond help. She sat on the couch slumped forward and using just about every muscle available to get her next breath. It was only a matter of time she would be too fatigued to breathe and her respirations would stop.

The patient had a look of panic on her face as she watched me organize my crew. Her family stood by helplessly watching and waiting. The clock was ticking. I needed to get her to the rig and hook her up to our CPAP device. Forcing air through the sealed mask would make her effort of breathing easier and possibly improve her recovery in the hospital.

"Can you talk," I ask the woman, as I wait for the bed to arrive. She is barely able to get one word out. Time seems to slow down. It feels like the guys are taking forever to return with the gurney. I didn't want to have a conversation with the woman. I wanted to get moving, now.

Finally, the gurney arrives.

"Alright, let's pick her up and go," I direct the volunteers. "Sit her up as high as you can. Get some pillows and blankets behind her."

The woman had wheezing throughout with each breath as she took small gasps trying to force air through the tightness in her lungs. As we wheeled her up the uneven rock driveway, her head bobbled with the movement.

"We're going to have to bag her in the rig," I tell the volunteer helping me push the gurney.

As we enter the back of the rig, I tell the responders, "I'll take two riders." My partner gets up front and takes off priority toward the hospital.

Everything proceeded quickly. I direct one of the volunteers to sit down at the head-end of the gurney as I hand him a bag valve mask.

He obtains a seal on the patient's face and assists each breath she takes in.

I tear open the bag to the continuous positive air pressure device. After assembling attachments to the mask, I toss the end of the oxygen tubing to the volunteer at the head. He attaches the oxygen tubing to the wall mounted supply and I seal the mask to the patient's face. The EMT cranks the oxygen delivery up to maximum flow.

With the patient's breathing being taken care of, I grab an intraosseous needle and drill it through the bone in her. The patient doesn't even budge. She is focused on her breathing.

I attach a bag of fluids to the IO needle and look up to check on the patient's improvement.

"Is that mask helping you breathe?" I ask. "Shake your head or give me thumbs up." I pray for a yes, but the look on her face tells me something is wrong.

She shakes her head "No."

"Do you feel it working?" I ask her.

She shakes her head "Yes."

Something didn't seem right. I had used CPAP successfully countless times in the past, but this time it wasn't the same. I place my ear close to the mask to listen for airflow. The ambient noise in the rig was deafening as we screamed down the highway with sirens blasting and a diesel motor racing, but I couldn't help but think that the mask didn't sound very loud.

I check for a seal of the mask against the patient's face and it is properly seated. I confirm with the firefighter that oxygen is running and he verifies.

"Check the connection again," I tell the volunteer. He pushes the end of the oxygen tubing further onto the regulator attachment, but there is no change.

"It's good," he conforms.

I look back and the patient is unconscious. Her head is flopped forward and body buckled, only being held up by the seatbelts.

"Shit! She's unconscious! Lay her down," I order.

I swap positions with the volunteer seated at the head of the gurney and quickly rip off the CPAP mask. I grab the bag valve and begin breathing for the patient.

"Check a pulse," I tell the rider. He reaches in and finds one. It's time to intubate.

I grab my kit and insert the laryngoscope blade into the patient's mouth. After visualizing the vocal cords, I start pushing the tube through. Even though the woman was unconscious, she still gagged on the tube as it was being placed. Her vocal cords begin to spasm from the foreign body introduced and won't let me pass the breathing tube.

Damn! You've got to be kidding me! How does she have a gag reflex? I don't have enough time to draw meds. This woman is going to code if we wait any longer, I tell myself.

But, there was no other option. I swap positions with the volunteer once again. He begins breathing for the patient while I draw up the medication. The process may have taken a minute, but the agonizing event seemed to last forever. After pushing the paralyzing agent, the vocal cords relaxed and I was able to pass the tube with no problem.

For the remainder of the transport, we kept a careful watch on the patient's vitals. She remained alive but unresponsive as we entered the emergency department.

My partner and I took a few hours to get back in service. A healthy break was necessary after a critical call. It gave time to debrief and critique. From there, you could clear your head and find areas to improve care for your next patient. Otherwise, mentally, you were never really on the next call.

My main focus was to troubleshoot the failed CPAP device. We assemble a new mask and seal it to my face. Without any air flowing,

I could really feel the resistance the mask created, even with normal breathing.

"Turn on the oxygen," I tell my partner so I could breathe easier. He attaches the tubing to wall-mounted regulator. The airflow through the mask does not improve.

"That's fucked up," I tell my partner as I detach the mask. "It's no wonder she went out on us. This shit doesn't work. I can barely feel the oxygen flowing through."

We go through all of the possibilities again as to why our device was failing.

"It's turned up all the way," I confirm.

"Yep, it's maxed out," my partner says. "Maybe it's something with the wall mount."

We both take a look at the setup. He pushes the regulator into the housing on the wall and finds it properly seated. He adjusts the settings knob and finds it tight and sealed. He then grabs the adapter, which provides a connection between large regulator and the oxygen tubing.

"Dude, the fucking tree is loose," he says, referring to the adapter.

"Are you serious?"

"Yeah. Check it out!"

We screw the 'tree' adapter tight and run oxygen through the CPAP one more time. Immediately there is a rush of air through the mask.

"Wow! I can feel that now!" I cry out. "That's crazy!"

The solution was so simple. It was right there. We had touched the connection, but failed to find the problem in time.

I sat there shaking my head. "God damn! We pretty much suffocated her."

THE CLOSEST UNIT

Guilt slowly seeped in. As much as I had tried to ignore what had happened, the thought that we caused a woman to suffer until she went unconscious kept eating away at me. There was nothing I could do to change it. There was no getting over it. The accumulation of misery I experienced as a result was weighing heavy on my emotions. I never felt sad. Those emotions were tucked away too tight. Instead, I expressed anger and resentment. I couldn't get the look of the woman's face out of my mind. Each time I felt her cry for help, I remembered how we failed to provide the most basic duty. *Primum Non Nocere*.

   Alcohol helped me cope with the stress, but it was actually the alcohol which helped me release my suppressed feelings. On the way back from a party with my wife driving, I broke into tears. I never wanted to hurt anyone. I wanted to help. She was relying on me and I failed her.

Even though I knew I had helped people in my career, the satisfaction was still not there. It never was. My focus was constantly on the negative. I would critique what went wrong and blame myself for simple problems. Even if I ultimately helped someone, the process never ran perfectly and for that I took personal responsibility.

I had a strong drive to help others. The urge to be there when aid was needed was intense. Even though the job was wearing on me mentally, I still strived to be out on the streets attempting to make a difference. It was like a drug. I knew it was bad for me, but I still couldn't get enough.

We were returning to our station from a previous call when we got toned out for a nearby assault in progress. After responding for a few blocks, we arrived at the designated staging area. This would put us in position to be available the moment police had the situation under control.

We sat quietly for what seemed like forever. Police units in the area were busy handling more severe situations and were unable to respond immediately. As we listen to the radio traffic around the area, a structure fire was reported only blocks from our location.

We pay close attention to the radio traffic, intrigued to find out if the reported fire was legitimate or not. We figured it would provide entertainment as we waited for police to secure our scene. As we sat eagerly in an empty parking lot with no end in sight, the first incoming engine company reports smoke showing from the residence.

"Engine eleven is on scene of a working structure fire, smoke and flames from the Charlie/Delta side, we will be performing an interior attack."

I pictured the scene in my head. I missed my time with the fire department. Volunteering with my dad and brother was one of the best experiences of my life. They were happy memories which would last forever. I remembered entering a smoky house, suited with bunker gear, and watching as the search team brought out a victim from a back bedroom. It was a rush like no other and one I surely missed.

A garbled voice with heavy breathing comes over the radio.

"Command, we have two victims. We will be coming out the alpha side. Send me another medic unit."

"They have victims!" I tell my partner. "We have to get off this call."

He gets on the radio and requests an estimated time of arrival of our responding police unit. We are told that aid had been refused and we can return to available status.

My heart is pumping with excitement. I want nothing more than to be there at the fire scene attending to the victims. Both were reported to be conscious but having trouble breathing due to burns in their airway. Racing with anticipation and the overwhelming urge to be involved, we put ourselves available and await orders to respond to the fire scene.

Finally, the dispatcher returns with our orders. We don't get sent on the fire. Instead, we get dispatched across town for an older male who passed out.

My partner gets back on the radio, "Dispatch, we are a only couple of blocks from the fire. Would you like us to respond?"

"Negative, we already have a unit assigned. Continue on your response."

"He's giving us a God damn medical!" I shout. The unit which was initially dispatched was responding from the other end of our district. "We're not even fucking close to that! We're the closest unit to the fire!"

"Received," my partner grabs the microphone and shoves it back into its holder in anger.

There was nothing we could do. We respond to the syncopal episode while listening to the fire scene progress. Our elderly patient had passed out and was worried about his heart, so we gave him a ride to the hospital.

We treated the patient respectably. He deserved it. He did not cause us to miss out on attending more critical victims. Still, I was frustrated beyond belief. On our way to the hospital, my partner updates me on the fire scene. "They've asked for another priority transport. I guess they still had one more victim inside."

I quietly shake my head. I bite my lip and hold down the anger that I wanted to release. I had to maintain my composure in the face of my patient. He was supposed to be my most important priority right now, but I couldn't help but think about the fire victims. Inside, I was filling with rage. I felt like I was going to explode if I didn't get it out.

I leaned my head into the front cab and talk to my partner quietly. "This is fucking bullshit. This is what kills me. I can't stand this system! We should have been on that call. We were three blocks away!"

"I know, man, but you really don't want to be a part of those anyways. It's too much paperwork," he tells me in an attempt to settle me down. I wasn't concerned about the work involved and he knew that. I felt a burning desire to help others and that flame was smothered by the very system that was put in place to manage those emergencies.

"I just feel that we could have actually done something, you know. I mean, you know me. I don't normally bitch about *not* doing calls."

"I hear you," he tells me.

At the end of the transport, our patient thanked us. I didn't deserve it. My attention was not on him.

The emergency services lounge was packed full of responders from the fire, all sharing stories of the intense scene. After dropping off my patient, I did not talk to anyone. Instead of hanging out in the lounge as I normally would, I sat in the front seat of my ambulance alone and tried to write my report.

I couldn't focus. My mind kept trailing to the decision dispatch made. As I sat there groaning about the situation, I watch my supervisor walk out from the emergency entrance. I decided to approach him.

"Hey!" I shout, getting his attention as I quickly walk up on him. He stops, turns back and looks. I have a look of anger in my eyes. I get close and irritably ask him, "Is there a reason dispatch didn't send us on that call when we are *three* blocks away!"

He shakes his head and shrugs his shoulders as he walks off. "I don't know what to tell you, Stone."

"It's frustrating!" I shout to him. I shake my head in disbelief. "It's..." He continues to walk away.

Fuck this place! I am so sick of it!

Ambulance Drivers

Stress and frustration from the job had overpowered my desire to help and was driving me out of the field. I moved down to part-time status to make life bearable. My attitude at work was destructive. I was bitter and burned out. I became the image I strived not to be when I was new. I wanted out of the field, but couldn't find it in me to quit. Deep inside, there was a caring, compassionate soul. But my career was turning me into someone I despised.

There are moments in life where you feel you were put in a certain place and time for a reason. This was one of those times.

"Respond priority for shortness of breath." The radio traffic interrupts a well-deserved break on what was turning out to be a busy day.

"En route," I respond. My partner flips on the emergency signals and heads to the small neighboring town just outside of our district. This area was covered by its own volunteer fire service. Most of the responders were young, timid kids who threw a fire department t-shirt over a pair of blue jeans to attend a response. Even though presentation was lacking in their department, the members were dedicated to the task and strived to be the best.

We roll up to the address. A young volunteer rushes out the front door waving us down. *Yes, yes, we know where you guys are, thank you for the help*, I sarcastically say to myself. His rushed presentation doesn't get me hyped up. I expect a more frantic scene when we respond with this department. They were small in size and didn't get the call volume we were used to in the city. Most of the members were just starting out and lacked real-world experience. It reminded me of when I was a volunteer. I was always hyped up and ready for action. Now, my calm manner on scene had people questioning if I even recognized an emergency was actually occurring.

"Just grab the medical bag and monitor for now," I tell my partner. "We're close if we need any more equipment."

I step out from the passenger seat and the volunteer runs up to me. He almost looks out of breath and his face is full of excitement.

"We need your AED!" he shouts, frantically.

"Okay, we're bringing it," I tell him. I look back at my partner. "Grab the suction, too."

We carry the equipment inside. As I enter the doorway, I notice the husband is standing in the corner of the living room with his hand covering his mouth. Within a moment, the backs of two firefighters emerge from the hallway in front of me. It is the chief and a volunteer dragging the patient down the hallway by her legs.

The initial rush of nerves that usually occurred didn't happen. I quickly set my monitor down on the floor and gave them a hand to navigate the body around the sharp hallway corner. We pull her into the living room where we will have enough space to work. The woman looks to be in her sixties. She is blue in the face and not breathing. I start cutting the clothing off.

"Alright, what's the story?" I ask the crew as I turn on my monitor and start placing the defibrillator pads.

"She was in the bathroom talking to us just a minute ago but then she passed out. Last we checked she still had a pulse."

"She's not breathing. Someone start bagging her," I direct. "Does she have a pulse now?"

"Well she did..." I get in response.

"How about now? Does she have a pulse now?" I demand. The volunteer checks for a pulse at the neck.

"I don't feel a pulse," she reports back.

"Alright, get on the chest then. Start CPR," I tell the crew.

After a brief moment, I order the crew to stop compressions and I take a look at the rhythm. It's a slow and organized, but not producing a pulse.

"Okay, continue CPR," I tell them and the crew resumes.

My partner asks, "Do you want me to get the gurney?"

I had run many cardiac arrest calls in my career and understood the mortality rate associated with such a heart rhythm. This was a non-shockable rhythm which gave even less hope that the woman would make it. In my head, I knew the probability of us pronouncing her dead on scene was high. There was no need to prepare for transport.

I tell my partner, "No. She's in idioventricular. It's PEA. Let's work her here and see how she does."

I felt calm and reassured as I worked through the motions. I was able to think clearly and systematically. Each step progressed effortlessly and without any deliberation in thought. Everything just came to me. It was almost going perfectly.

I grab an intraosseous needle from the kit and tell my partner to prepare an Epinephrine injection. As I started drilling the needle into the woman's leg, it met resistance. I push harder and feel the bone needle bend.

"What the fuck?" I whisper to myself, more in amazement than frustration. I remained calm and decided to try for an IV instead. The IV goes in fluently. My partner hands me the epinephrine and I push it into her veins.

After two minutes of CPR, I have the crew stop compressions once again so I can take another look at the monitor. The rhythm changed. The once slow, ineffective beat was now tight and fast, showing her whole heart was now pumping effectively.

"She's in normal sinus now. Check a pulse again," I tell the girl.

She places fingers on the woman's neck and looks up in amazement. "I think she might have one. I'm not sure." Oddly enough, it reminded me of myself during the first cardiac arrest call I ran as a volunteer.

"Okay, so there is a pulse or not?" I ask for confirmation.

The chief steps in to double check. "Yeah, there's something there but it's really faint. Do you want us to continue CPR or hold off?" he asks.

I weigh the options in my head. *What the hell,* I think. *What's the worst that can happen? She's probably close to slipping back into full arrest anyways. Another round of CPR won't hurt.*

"Yeah, go ahead. We'll do one more round of compressions."

I move up to the head of the patient to intubate. As I assemble my equipment, I hear the sound of a breath.

Is she breathing on her own? I wonder. The rate of improvement amazed me. I have the crew stop compressions shortly so I can confirm. The woman takes another breath. I check the pulse at the neck and it is strong. I reach down to the wrist and feel for a distal pulse to gauze a possible blood pressure and it is faint but still present. *She's breathing. She has pulses. She has a blood pressure. We're transporting!*

"Hold off on CPR, guys. I'm going to tube her."

I shout to my partner, "Grab the gurney and backboard now! We're transporting!"

I direct my attention back to the volunteers. "Get ready guys, as soon as I drop this tube, we're going to load her up and get going. I'm taking two riders."

As I insert the laryngoscope blade deep in the patient's throat, I can see the vocal cords moving with each breath she takes. I push past a slight gag reflex and insert the breathing tube. My partner returns with the bed, the patient gets loaded, and we haul off toward the hospital.

After delivering the patient, I walk out of the emergency room with a sense of astonishment. I didn't know how to respond to it. For once, everything seemed to go right. In a way, it was kind of eerie.

A few months later, I got a phone call from our clinical department.

"Mr. Stone," the voice identifies me.

"Yes," I reluctantly answer, wondering why the clinical department would possibly want to talk to me. They frequently dealt with quality assurance issues so when they called it was not a good sign.

"Remember that cardiac arrest patient you had a few months ago?" She continues to describe the call.

"Yes, I do." The worries went away. I had no doubt that call went well.

"I just wanted to call and congratulate you. Your efforts resulted in a life saved. We just got notification that the patient walked out of the hospital with no neurological deficits."

"Oh my God, that's great news!" I say, relieved in many ways. "Thank you for letting me know."

"I know you guys don't always get good news, but I just wanted to let you know you are doing a great job out there and to keep up the good work!"

"Thank you!"

HANDS OF AN ANGEL

Scientific research suggests the standard that becomes printed in our textbooks, but we never see a "textbook patient." The research indicates what is probable. But, in the field we experience the unexplainable.

I had many doctors tell me to my face that what I was reporting was impossible.

"There is no way she could have recovered that fast. You must have misinterpreted your initial exam," or, "Are you sure that is what you saw? People don't deteriorate that quickly. You must have missed something," they would tell me.

They looked to the textbook for answers, but my experience had me believe there was something greater out there effecting our lives.

As I was struggling to cope with stress in my life, I began looking for something to turn it around. I happened across a book, written by a local physician named Jeffery Long. The book is titled "Evidence of the Afterlife." What was written by those who had experienced a near-death experience was amazing and put life into perspective.

As I read through the stories, a piece stood out which brought chills down my spine. The story involved a surgical process where the patient had a minimal chance of survival. During the surgery, the man had a near-death experience. As the team worked to revive him, he saw the scene from a perspective outside of his body.

The man, in spiritual form, watched as the surgeons performed on his body. Standing behind each surgeon was an angel who was guiding their hands during the procedure. After the patient recovered, the surgeon remarked how it had been the best surgery he had ever performed. Everything went perfect and he knew exactly what to do in the moment without hesitation.

I immediately recalled my saved victim. I remember the moment I entered the room and saw the frightened husband. I remembered watching the firefighters drag the body of the dead woman down the hall. We were expecting a simple difficulty breathing call, but instead were thrown the most critical patient.

The most satisfying memory was how I felt upon having patient contact. It was different than any other call. I was calm. My mind worked fluently. I effortlessly guided my team to the right plan and we executed it to perfection.

This woman was meant to live. I wondered if her angels had helped me perform in the same way. Everything felt identical to what I was reading. I had made the same exact statement to my wife that the surgeon made in his writing: "Everything went perfect."

There are moments in life where you feel you were put in a certain place and time for a reason. I don't think I was put there to save that woman's life. Anyone else could have done it better. I was not the best chance she had for survival. I was put in that situation to become a better person.

I had seen all aspects of field medicine and it had driven me to burnout. I could no longer stand patients and had lost compassion, even for those with legitimate complaints. I couldn't stand the hospital staff due to their constant negative attitudes towards us. The stress from the job had overcome me and led me down a path of destruction.

This woman came into my life to save me. She gave me understanding of who I wanted to become and the path I needed to take to get back to where I was. She showed me God working in all of us and how we had the potential to touch the entire world.

With the understanding that I had made such a positive difference in someone else's life, I finally came content with taking the next step in my own. After ten years in the emergency medical field, I decided to end my service as a Paramedic. It was an incredibly tough decision, but one I ultimately knew I needed to make.

Although the constant exposure to that side of life is over, I still have its effects. I easily get angered or frustrated as a result of feeling out of control because it reminds me of the calls where things didn't go well. I easily get flustered with multiple details due to feeling overwhelmed during other people's emergencies. I get anxiety over the sounds of my kids playing throughout the house because their screaming sounds like a tragic scene. I constantly look for the problem in situations and focus on the negative because that's what I was trained to do.

The world has an interesting way of creating balance. For every bad thing that happens, there seems to be an equal amount of good that comes from it. It takes experiencing pain and misery in life to really appreciate what good the world has to offer. It provides contrast between your life now and the way it could be.

Life is meant to be lived to the fullest. It should be spent creating memories with those you love. We are here to spread love and joy to those we cross paths with. Every good deed, no matter how big or small, has a ripple effect and changes more lives than we could ever imagine. This strengthens our spirit and has the power to make the world a better place.

WHAT'S THE BEST CALL YOU'VE EVER HAD?

Many people have approached me and asked what's the worst or most disgusting thing I've ever seen. They've asked me what's the most tragic call I've ever run. But, no one has ever asked about my best call. I've experienced the unsightly. I've also experienced calls full of wonderful emotions.

One of the greatest experiences I had was the opportunity to work directly alongside my brother. He had obtained his medic a year before I entered my program. At the time, I was nearing the end of training but still had to function at a basic level on the job.

Due to policies in place, relatives were not allowed to work together on a unit, although a one-time exception had been made. The city of Denver announced it required additional units to cover an anticipated heavy load of emergency responses due to the Democratic National Convention and we were selected to support.

From hopping over curbs driving priority through downtown traffic to fighting a combative seizure patient and stabilizing a critical respiratory distress victim, I was able push out of my scope slightly under Mike's supervision. It brought us back to the days of volunteering and gave us one final hoorah together.

But, my all time favorite call was not action packed or full of gore. It did not involve successful scene management or superior skill. It did not involve saving a life. My all-time favorite call was an inner-facility transport for an elderly woman who was being sent back to her nursing home.

We arrived to the floor of the hospital to pick up the patient. She was a German woman with a thick accent and severe dementia. The nurse tells us, "She is the sweetest woman in the world. You guys are going to love her."

The woman could not remember one minute from the next. During our transport, she repeatedly tells me, "I just love you guys. You guys are so sweet." After fifteen minutes of being filled with warm sentiment, we wheeled her to her room. Bursting out from her room came two small puppies. She insisted we pet them and enjoy their playfulness.

After we dropped off the sweetest woman in the world, the staff of the unit showed us to the complementary ice cream and popcorn bar. I topped my cup of ice cream with a chocolate chip cookie and headed back to the rig to write my report.

Today Was a Good Day

[Verse One]
Just got on shift in the morning gotta thank God
I don't know but today seems kinda odd
Med-comm had no calls, no falls
And partner brought in breakfast with pulled hog
I got my drug box, but kinda wigged out
When dispatch tried to send us on a call before we get out
Closer unit hooked it up as we hit the door
Thinking will I make it another twenty-four
I gotta go do a rig check and I'm shocked
'Cause when I get in back I find that it's all stocked
Hit the streets, stop at a red light
Looking in my mirror not a bum in sight
And everything is alright
I got a beep from sup, we're fully staffed all night
Called up the homies and I ask the bunch
Which place are y'all going to get some lunch?
Ordering food on shift is usually trouble
Got the platter and they served it up on the double
Freaky fast like Jimmy John's I have to say
I can't believe, today was a good day

[Verse Two]
Drivin' past a scene to see what's happening
Didn't even get no static from the Captain
Cause just the other day them fools tried turfin'
Saw the medic unit and we rolled right past 'em
No stressing, made it through Tacoma's streets with no direction
'cause they marked the intersections
Ran with Browns Point Fire, tapped out a CPR in progress
Got to play real medic
Pump the chest, pump the chest, pump the chest, shock 'em
Roll out with a circle of basics and watch me drop the tube

Then Epi, Amio, Epi, Amio, Epi
Transporting priority to St Joe's
Picked up a faint pulse
Head started bucking, now I'm hollerin' Vecuron'
Plus no regular I know called 911 to whisk 'em away
Today was a good day

[Verse Three]
It's Friday and I got paid
Just got that vein I'd been trying to stick for the 12th day
It's ironic, pushed the Haldol with no dystonic
Then filled him up with isotonic
Tight restraints on a combative patient
Ran the equation and pushed the sedation
M.A.D. got the drugs deep, so deep up his nose put his ass to sleep
Got to post V.A.
And didn't hesitate to get some sleep while getting paid
Four hours later then we're coastin'
Pop the Rockstar, sip the potion
With no emotion
Stomach is churning while were inbound
Dropped by T.G. to raid the lounge
Today no nursing home geriatrics
Didn't even need to gurney swap for bariatric
No hospitals on divert status
Two in the morning, running street addicts
Dropped the OPA in 'cause his tongue went limp
And started bagging this unconscious pimp
Pushed the Narcan with no throwing up
Halfway done and our fuel tank's still filled up
Today I didn't even have to decon delay
I got to say it was a good day

PICTURES

Recruit Academy

FATHER AND SONS

BROTHERS

Volunteer Firefighter

Extrication Training

Downtime

Paramedic
School

Non-Injury

Monday Morning Quarterback

(After Party)

Off the Clock Medicine

(Passed Out While Pregnant)

AMBULANCE DRIVERS)

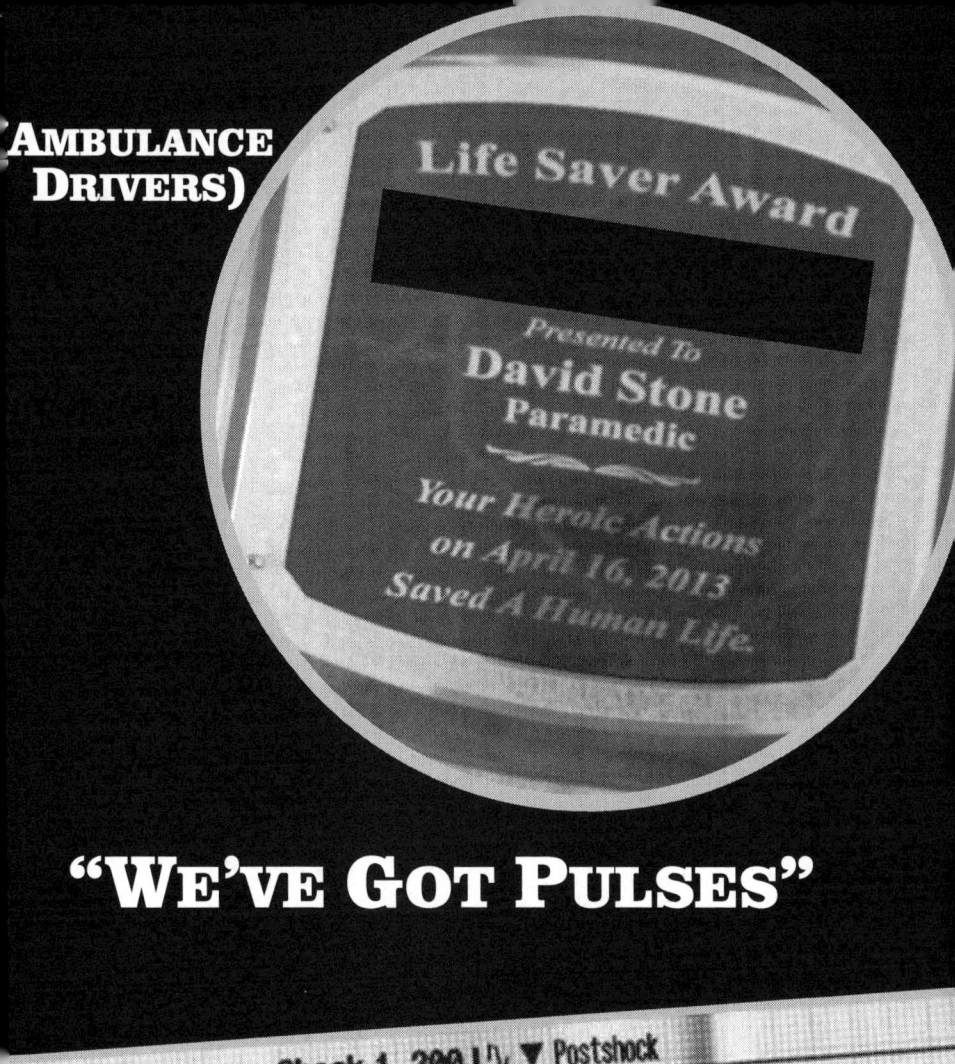

Life Saver Award

Presented To
David Stone
Paramedic

Your Heroic Actions
on April 16, 2013
Saved A Human Life.

"We've Got Pulses"

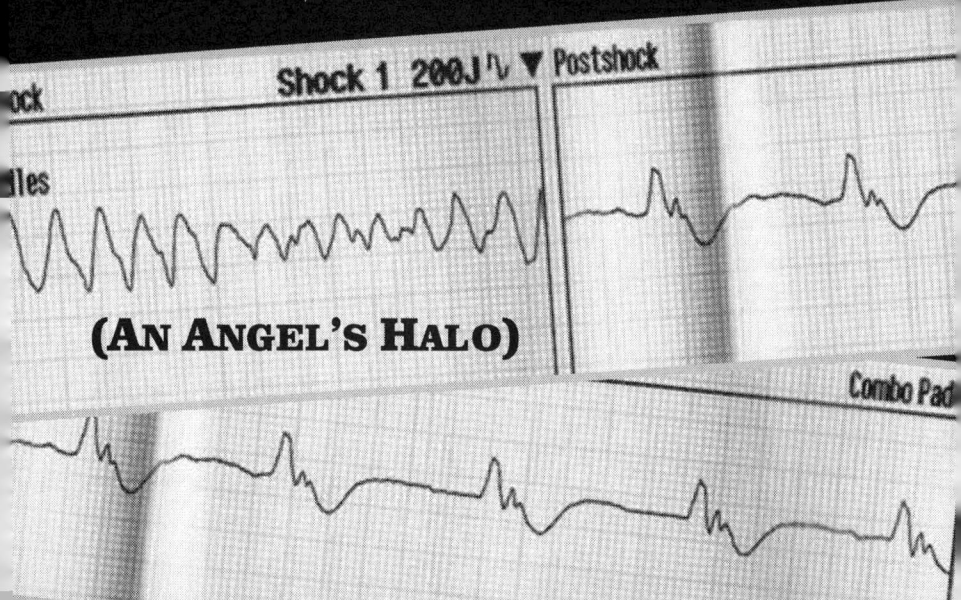

Shock 1 200J ▼ Postshock

(An Angel's Halo)

Combo Pad

Made in the USA
Lexington, KY
19 April 2017